RUGBY'S STRANGEST® MATCHES

Other titles in the STRANGEST series

Football's Strangest Matches
Law's Strangest Cases
London's Strangest Tales

Titles coming soon

Cricket's Strangest Matches
Golf's Strangest Rounds
Kent's Strangest Tales
Medicine's Strangest Cases
Motor-racing's Strangest Races
Running's Strangest Tales
Shakespeare's Strangest Tales
Teachers' Strangest Tales
Tennis's Strangest Matches

RUGBY'S STRANGEST® MATCHES

Extraordinary but true stories
from over a century of rugby

JOHN GRIFFITHS

PORTICO

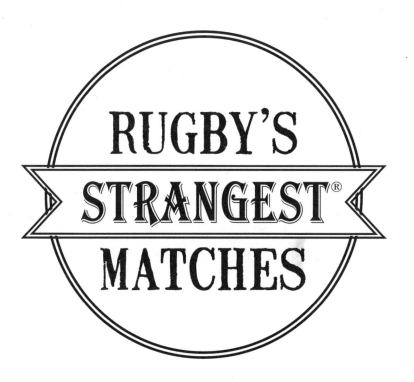

Published in the United Kingdom in 2016 by
Portico
43 Great Ormond Street
London
WC1N 3HZ

An imprint of Pavilion Books Company Ltd

ISBN 978-1-91023-287-3

A CIP catalogue record for this book is available from the British Library.

10 9 8 7 6 5 4 3 2

Reproduction by Colourdepth UK
Printed and bound by Bookwell, Finland

This book can be ordered direct from the publisher at www.pavilionbooks.com, or try your local bookshop.

CONTENTS

INTRODUCTION

Rugby's Strangest Matches describes some of the game's most curious occasions of the past 145 years. Any unusual team or individual performance, or any occurrence during or surrounding a match that was a clear departure from the normal run of things, has been regarded as strange and thus worthy of inclusion.

This collection of true stories includes the match when an Irish international player arranged his marriage in order to qualify for leave of absence to play against England, the occasion when a team of top English soccer players beat their rugby counterparts at the 15-a-side game, the game where an almost complete unknown played for his country due to an administrative mistake, and the match where a well-known referee was sent off.

Naturally, 'strangeness' is subjective depending on the circumstances at the time and one's own point of view. Therefore there may well be some argument relating to what has been included and what has been left out. For the most part, the stories concentrate on the games played at senior international level because these attracted more attention and wider media coverage. No doubt there are many others, which would qualify for inclusion, but for which there are no reported accounts.

The majority of the work is based on newspaper research and personal memories. My first debt of gratitude is therefore to the recorders of the game, past and present, for setting down what otherwise would have been lost for all time. In particular, the personal recollections and lighter asides, in word and in print, of Viv Jenkins, Frank Keating, Ian Malin, David Hands, John Mason, Steve Jones, Rob Wildman, Brendan Gallagher, Patrick Lennon and Mick Cleary have helped to illuminate many of the stories appearing in this collection.

Elsewhere, behind the scenes, I owe a debt of gratitude to three old friends, Tim Auty of Leeds, Geoff Miller in New Zealand and Tony Lewis of Pyle in South Wales for suggesting ideas and forwarding copies of cuttings from their own archives. Finally, thanks go to Jeremy Robson for commissioning the original edition, and to Lorna Russell at Robson Books and more recently Nicola Newman and Katie Hewett at Pavilion for their skilful and patient management of the project.

John Griffiths

DR ALMOND'S WORDS OF WISDOM

EDINBURGH, MARCH 1871

Rugby union's first international was always going to be a strange match. The background to the occasion gives some insight into the unusual circumstances surrounding international sport nearly 130 years ago.

There had been a soccer international between England and a 'Scotland XI' in November 1870. England's win by a goal to nil angered those north of the Border, where it was contended that the only connection the losers had with 'their' country was a liking for Scotch whisky. The Scots asserted that the principal version of football played at their schools and universities was rugby and they issued a challenge to England to pick a side for an international rugby match to be staged at Raeburn Place, Edinburgh, in March 1871.

The English accepted and their selected 20 (13 forwards and seven backs) got down to earnest preparations for the big match. Typical of the training undertaken by their players was the regimen of one John Henry Clayton, a forward from the Liverpool club. Weighing in at more than 17st (108kg), his training makes fascinating reading. For a month before the match he ran 4 miles (6.4km) every morning, his large Newfoundland dog 'making the pace'. A 4-mile (6.4-km) horseback ride took him to his Liverpool office where he put in a 12-hour day, 8a.m. to 8p.m., before making the return journey home to a dinner of underdone-beef-and-beer. He laid claim to a 'frugal and strenuous life otherwise'.

Travelling arrangements were in stark contrast to those of today. England travelled north on Saturday night (for the Monday match) in third-class rail carriages with bare board seats. Arriving at dawn next day, they took baths before finding accommodation. All travelling and hotel expenses were met by the players themselves.

The next day dawned bright and clear and more than 2,000 spectators arrived to see Scotland win on a pitch that was judged narrow compared with English standards. The game was largely a protracted maul – imagine rugby today being played among 40 men, most of them forwards – and several of the laws peculiar to the Scottish version of rugby were adopted. England, in short, were clearly playing against the odds. Even so, in the two halves of 50 minutes each, their backs impressed Scottish observers with their willingness to run with the ball.

Scoring by points was not introduced to rugby football until the late 1880s and at the time of this inaugural international the only way a match could be won was by a majority of goals: drop goals or converted tries. (Penalty goals would not sully rugby's scoring until more than 20 years later.) Tries alone were of no value. They simply enabled sides to 'try' for a goal.

Scotland scored the only goal of the match early in the second half. They succeeded in pushing a scrummage over the England goal line and to Angus Buchanan, who grounded the ball, fell the distinction of scoring the first try in international rugby. But not before England had disputed its legality.

A lengthy and by all accounts heated debate ensued before the try was allowed to stand. Referees did not appear in matches until the mid-1870s so appeals were heard by umpires (later known as touch judges). The umpire who awarded the try, which was converted into a goal by William Cross with a fine kick, was Scotland's Dr Almond, the well-known headmaster of Loretto.

The wisdom behind his allowing the score was later set in print: 'Let me make a confession,' he wrote. 'I do not know whether the decision which gave Scotland the try from which the winning goal was kicked was correct in fact. When an umpire is in doubt, I think he is justified in deciding against the side which makes most noise. They are probably in the wrong.' Both sides added later tries but in the absence of successful conversions, Scotland held their controversial lead. Accounts of the match refer to their superior fitness so it seems reasonable to assume that the better side won.

IRISH CHAOS

THE OVAL, FEBRUARY 1875

Ireland's entry into international rugby in 1875 was surrounded by chaos. The Irish Football Union was formed in November the previous year but, much to the annoyance of the Belfast rugby clubs, none of their representatives were present. That same month in Belfast, a representative Dublin club rugby XV played their Belfast counterparts in a forerunner of what is now the Leinster–Ulster interprovincial matches. There was great interest in the match, as it was perceived as a trial for the forthcoming international against England.

The Belfast men triumphed in difficult conditions and then proceeded to give the vanquished a wigging. The Ulstermen underlined their annoyance at not having been invited to the formation of the Union by proceeding to form their own North of Ireland Union in direct opposition to the Dubliners.

However, with the fixture against England in London looming, the two parties eventually reached a compromise. It was diplomatically decided that both should nominate ten players to the team of 20. But not much thought went into the selection process.

There was no communication between the two unions about the positions players would occupy. Indeed, many of them had never seen one another before. As a result, there was chaos. Backs were made to play in forward positions and vice-versa. Two of those chosen to play did not even appear and it was no surprise that Ireland were penned deep in their own half for the entire match.

The trenchant Irish critic of the day, Jacques MacCarthy, wrote: 'The whole lot were immaculately innocent of training.' They were also unfit and, it was reckoned, would have been well beaten by a fourth-rate London club. In fairness, it should be pointed out that rugby in Ireland in the 1870s was played by teams of 15-a-side and the Irish forwards who met England at the Oval were far too light and inexperienced to play effectively at the long-drawn-out mauling game that was a feature of 20-a-side rugby.

Ireland were also found wanting in the drop-kicking department. The technique was virtually unknown in their club circles and when Richard Walkington, their full-back, was entrusted with a drop-out he was unable to propel the ball farther than 10 yards (9.1m).

Even so, despite their inadequacies, Ireland only went down by a goal, a dropped goal and a try to nil. That, however, did not prevent the football correspondent of the Field from declaring: 'I could whip up 20 Irishmen resident in London who would make hares of this pseudo-Irish 20.'

THE FIRST XVs

THE OVAL, FEBRUARY 1877

Those who turned up to see the international match between England and Ireland in 1877 would have regarded the events of the next 80 minutes as quite unusual.

Up to this time, internationals had been played between teams of 20 players a side, normally lined out with three full-backs, a solitary three-quarter back, three half-backs and 13 forwards. Most of the time the ball was lost in scrums and mauls comprising 26 forwards. Backs would have been very lucky to get their hands on the ball and attacking movements among them were virtually non-existent.

On the rare occasions when a player was able to make a run with the ball, one of the vast number of opponents invariably collared him. The laws of the game at the time required a player so held to call 'Down'. That was the signal for the two packs to gather around the player, who then placed the ball on the floor. A scrum then formed around the ball and the object was for one set of forwards to try to drive it through and break away down field, usually with a dribble.

Such scrums were protracted affairs because there was no heeling or wheeling. Sides coming away with the ball left opponents lying on the ground in their wake. Brawn rather than brain was the order of the day.

Mindful that the rugby held little spectacle for anybody other than those who had played it, the law-making authorities began experimenting with ways to speed up the game. In 1875, Oxford and Cambridge pioneered the 15-a-side game and 15 months later the reduced number was first adopted for international matches when England hosted Ireland at Kennington Oval, home of the Surrey Cricket Club.

'The ball naturally made its appearance sooner from the diminished number of forwards, though the scrummages were still of formidable length owing to the methods then employed,' it was noted, after England had beaten the Irish by two goals and two tries to nil.

The England team was a light combination, selected, perhaps, with the 15-a-side occasion in mind. They were nimbler to the ball than their rivals and, observed the rugby correspondent of *The Times*, 'knew more of the science of the game.' The match was the first in which Albert Hornby, the Lancashire Test cricketer, appeared in an England rugby jersey. Aged nearly 30, he was the first rugby player to make use of the punt as a device for gaining ground. His kicks were an innovation as far as international rugby was concerned at the time and his effective methods attracted considerable comment. Hornby had attended Harrow School where, it was reported, the football game practised in his day was quite different from the version at Rugby School. The original Harrow game did not admit drop-kicking; indeed, the shape of the football was unsuited to such kicking. In its place, Hornby had developed the technique of punting and it was this kicking style which made him conspicuous throughout the match.

For the spectator in 1877, then, international rugby must have appeared to be a whole new ball game, with that year's England–Ireland fixture clearly marking the beginning of its modern version.

AND THERE WAS LIGHT

BROUGHTON, OCTOBER 1878

In the late 1870s bids were mounted by the fledgling electrical light companies to overturn the monopoly the gas companies held over urban street lighting. As Thomas Edison, in the United States, and Sir Joseph Swan, in Britain, perfected the design of the incandescent light bulb, less inspired experimenters were already using more primitive forms of electrical lighting.

Sport was an interested beneficiary of the new form of lighting with both football and rugby pioneering floodlit events in the winter of 1878–9. The first recorded rugby match under floodlights took place in the industrial north when Broughton entertained Swinton on 22 October, 1878. Two Gramme's Lights suspended from 30-ft (9.1-m) poles were used for illumination. Another match was staged in the Liverpool area the same month and the craze for 'illuminated matches' spread like wildfire as the electrical companies sought to promote their methods.

An interesting additional development in November was the use of a white ball for a match staged at Old Deer Park involving Surrey and Middlesex. Surrey won a match enlightened by four lamps driven by a couple of Siemens electro-dynamo machines.

Three months later on 24 February, 1879, the first floodlit game in Scotland took place at Hawick. Their local derby with Melrose, whom they defeated by a goal to nil, attracted a healthy crowd of 5,000 and a gate of £63. (It would have been much greater but for the fact that only one gate man was on duty and many poured through a hole in a perimeter fence without paying.) The power for the light came from two dynamos driven by steam engines, but the crowd had a shock when the parsimonious officials switched the power off immediately the match finished. Heavy snow had covered the pitch and surrounds and there was chaos as spectators skidded their way home in complete darkness.

Floodlit rugby for gate-money was actually prohibited by the Rugby Football Union 'as not in the interests of the game' in 1933. By the 1950s, however, Harlequins and Cardiff were staging a popular sequence of annual evening matches at the White City (before the Quins set up home at the Stoop) and there was a successful Floodlit Alliance series involving the major Welsh clubs in the 1960s.

Nowadays major internationals in the southern hemisphere are frequently staged as night games and the official world record attendance for a rugby union match was set when Australia played the All Blacks under the lights of the Olympic Stadium, Sydney, in July 2000. A crowd of 109,874 turned out to see the New Zealanders win a pulsating match 39–35.

LUCKY TO GET NIL

BLACKHEATH, FEBRUARY 1881

When the successful Welsh sides of the late 1960s and 1970s regularly beat England, and quite often by large scores, the joke in Wales was that the fixture would be dropped the next season – the implication being that England were unworthy of a full international match with mighty Wales.

Perhaps the Welsh were trying to get their own back for a slight against them by England nearly a hundred years earlier, when the sides first met in 1881 in one of the oddest matches ever involving Wales. It was a game that marked their entry into international rugby and took place before even the Welsh Rugby Union itself had been founded.

The man known as the 'father of Welsh Rugby', Richard Mullock, was the inspiration behind their maiden international. A mover and shaker of the South Wales Football Union, Mullock wrote to the Rugby Football Union in London early in the 1880–81 season, proposing an international rugby match with England. The English accepted the challenge and arranged a fixture for 19 February 1881 at Richardson's Field, Blackheath, which was then home to the famous Blackheath club.

If enterprise was one of Mr Mullock's strengths, organisation certainly wasn't. No trial match was staged and players were eventually chosen for the match by virtue of reputation. One of the last survivors of that Welsh side was Major Richard Summers of Haverfordwest. In an interview many years later he recalled that he was informally asked to play on the strength of his performances a couple of years earlier for his school, Cheltenham College, in matches against Cardiff and Newport. No formal invitations to play were sent out to the Welsh XV. Two did not turn up because they had not received instructions to attend and two bystanders, University undergraduates with tenuous Welsh links but who had travelled to London to see the match, had to be roped in to play for their country.

Mullock, however, did have the inspiration of clothing his side in scarlet jerseys and chose the Prince of Wales feathers as the emblem. Researchers have never uncovered his reasons for veering away from the black shirts with white leek that identified the uniform of the South Wales Football Club, the prototypes of representative Welsh rugby.

The Blackheath club used a local hostelry on the heath (the Princess of Wales, which remains a popular pub to this day) as its meeting and changing point for matches at the time. So, after mustering at the pub, the players of both countries changed and walked the half-mile (800m) or so across the Common to play.

The Welsh were hopelessly outplayed and must have over-indulged earlier whilst at the pub, for they went down by the staggering margin of seven goals, six tries and a dropped goal to nil (82–0 under modern scoring values). 'We were lucky to get nil,' said one of the Welsh team afterwards.

The Rugby Football Union *did* drop the fixture the following season, a glance through the record books showing that the Welsh only played against the North of England at Newport in January of the 1881–2 season. By then, though, the fall-out from the Blackheath disaster had led to Welsh rugby putting its house into some sort of order. The Union officially came into force in March 1881 and, although beaten at Newport, 'the good form shown by the Welshmen,' it was written, 'gained for them a place in the International fixtures [with England] of the future.'

THE LONG DISPUTED TRY

BLACKHEATH, MARCH 1884

The 1884 season was the first in which all four of the Home Unions played against each other. The Championship title depended on a head-on collision between the year's two unbeaten sides, England and Scotland, at Blackheath in March.

More than 8,000 made the trip to south-east London to see Scotland take the lead with a first-half try that was not converted. Soon after the interval came a disputed try. Scotland won a scrum near their line but one of their forwards, Charles Berry, fumbled the ball and knocked it backwards. Charles Gurdon picked it up for England, made a bee-line for the posts and fed it to fellow forward Richard Kindersley, who plunged over the line to claim a try.

The Scots, however, made an appeal to the referee that the try be disallowed. (Appeals by teams were part and parcel of the game in the 1880s.) They contended that *their* knock back had been illegal. But in England knock backs were perfectly legal and the point made by the English players to the referee, George Scriven of Ireland, was that in any case it was unfair that Scotland should benefit by their own mistake. (The rule relating to advantage did not enter the law book for another dozen years.) After ten minutes of earnest discussion, the referee ruled in England's favour and Wilfrid Bolton kicked the goal that sealed the match and with it the Championship.

After the game the Scots steadfastly refused to accept the ruling. The root of the problem was a straightforward difference in the reading of the laws, but why, they contended, should the Rugby Football Union (RFU) have sole rights over interpretation. The RFU's defence was more to the point: they argued that whatever the interpretation, the referee's decision was final.

But the two nations remained at loggerheads and cancelled their fixture for 1885. A year later the Irish Rugby Union proposed the formation of an International Board to frame the laws of the game and make rulings on disputes. Scotland and Wales were party to a meeting in Dublin where the Scots, two years after the event, finally accepted the outcome of their 1884 game.

England, unhappy about representation, boycotted the early meetings of the Board. In 1887 the Celtic nations passed a vote that effectively cold-shouldered the English from the International Championship for two years and it was not until 1890 that differences were finally resolved and England returned to the fold.

The International Board has remained rugby's leading administrative body ever since, but it is interesting to reflect that it might never have come into being but for Scotland's objections in that 1884 game with England.

ONE-ARMED PLAYER'S RECORD

NEWTON ABBOT, JANUARY 1886

When a player named Wakeham kicked 13 conversions from 13 attempts for Newton Abbot against Plymouth on 30 January 1886 it was claimed as a record for a club match in England.

The mark has long since been overtaken but one astonishing fact regarding Wakeham renders his record remarkable to this day: he had only one arm.

A HEROIC ACT

DUBLIN, FEBRUARY 1887

International rugby has been played on Lansdowne Road, Dublin, since 1878, making it the oldest arena in the world still staging Test matches. It is always worth going to experience the craic at the ground, whether Ireland win or lose, and one early occasion when the good-natured Irish had one of their own famous victories to enjoy was in February 1887, when they defeated England for the first time.

It was Ireland's opening game of the International Championship and, according to the critics of the day, they were determined to perform well against a team that had registered 11 wins and a draw in the opening dozen matches of rugby union's second-oldest international series.

Ireland selected a team that was the customary mix of youth and experience. Six of the chosen XV were former internationals, including their captain and half-back, Robert Warren. Among the new caps was big John Macauley, a forward, and Dolway Walkington, of whom it was said: 'in the dark his delicate sight tells terribly against him.' Fortunately for him the weather in Dublin that day was bright and clear and Walkington is reported to have enjoyed a blinder, helping to keep Ireland's line intact against an England side that had lost only twice in the previous ten years.

For Macauley, however, taking part in the game did not prove so straightforward. A miller's agent in Limerick, he had already used up his quota of holidays for the working year when he was called up for this match and consequently was refused further time off to play in the match. But Macauley was determined to take part and resorted to the only means left to him. He took the unusual step of getting married in order to obtain the necessary leave of absence. According to an Irish critic of the day: 'This was truly heroic, and his wife fully endorsed the enthusiasm.'

This heroism was amply rewarded. Ireland won by two converted tries to nil. English reports of the game were written in a tone that almost bordered on condescension. The blame for England's defeat was placed firmly on their forwards for 'allowing themselves to be hustled all over the field by their opponents'. The Irish, however, were ecstatic at beating England 'all ends up'. Macauley himself maintained a lifelong interest in Irish rugby up to the time of his death in his nineties in 1958. He served the Irish Rugby Union as its president in 1894–5, but his course of action in order to play in that match of 1877 does not seem to have been an inspiration to other Irish rugby players of the time. Up to the outbreak of war in 1914, only four married men had appeared in an Ireland rugby jersey.

There is, though, a tantalisingly cryptic comment on this match in the writings of Jacques MacCarthy, the Irish rugby writer whose reflections quite often appeared to be of the don't-let-the-facts-spoil-a-good-story school of journalism.

Reminiscing five years after the match, MacCarthy revealed: 'There are secrets about this match which must remain for the instruction of a future generation,' although he did divulge further that: 'Everything was arranged cut and dry, even to the very ball that was played with.'

Possibly the Irish met a day before the match to run through some tactics. In the 1880s, such an action would have been tantamount to an act of professionalism. Certainly the match reports of the game refer to the discipline of the well-drilled Irish forwards. But no-one seems to have put in print the real story behind this match.

TIME GENTLEMEN PLEASE?

WAKEFIELD, JANUARY 1889

Yorkshire won the first official English county championship in 1888–9, winning all six of their matches. They also played twice against the touring New Zealand Natives that season.

For the first match against the visitors at Manningham in December, the county inexplicably fielded what amounted to a second XV and were well beaten. For the return match at Wakefield a month later, the full strength of the county was called upon. William Cail, later a president and long-serving treasurer to the Rugby Football Union, acted as referee.

The county avenged its earlier defeat with a handsome victory over the tourists, but it was Mr Cail, with an episode of high farce, who provided the lasting memory of the match.

He had stopped his watch as usual when one of the Natives' forwards went down injured. After the player was passed fit to resume, however, Cail forgot to re-set his watch. Twenty minutes or so later, sensing the match must be drawing to its close, he glanced at his watch only to discover to his horror that it had stopped. He immediately called a halt to the game and dashed up into the press seats to appeal for an accurate measure regarding the time that had elapsed before returning to the pitch and resuming the game.

The crowd, content that their side had won comfortably (it might well have been different otherwise) found this very amusing. 'No less amusing,' it was later divulged, 'were the different replies made by the pressmen.'

A MAORI PROTEST

BLACKHEATH, FEBRUARY 1889

The tour of the 1888–9 New Zealand Native team was the most demanding in the game's history. The side, all of whom were native-born players, was known as the Maoris, although not all of them were full-blooded Maori. The playing party numbered 26 and assembled in May 1888 for a journey to Britain via Melbourne and Suez. The original itinerary took in a staggering 50-plus matches spread over six months. But, by the time the party broke up more than a year later, 107 matches had been played in England, Scotland, Ireland, Wales, Australia and New Zealand. Of these, 78 were won, six drawn and only 23 lost. In addition, the team played eight Aussie Rules matches during its three-week stay in Melbourne.

The British section of the tour opened in October with a match against Surrey County. In its preview of the match, the *Daily Telegraph*, long before the days of political correctness, told its readers, 'The Maoris have progressed since Captain Cook found the neatly tattooed ancestors of our visitors eating each other in the bush.'

The tourists won handsomely before a crowd of some 5,000, which included most of the touring Australian cricketers who had a month or so earlier lost the Ashes series to an England side led by Dr W.G. Grace. The match was refereed by Rowland Hill, the secretary of the Rugby Football Union, and as the game had passed uneventfully, the tourists took with a pinch of salt the warnings of the Aussie cricketers that they could expect difficulties with English referees.

Those warnings would haunt the Maoris four months later during the international against England at Blackheath. The referee for the match was again Rowland Hill, but this time the match was far from uneventful.

Play was even for the first quarter but, before half-time, England scored two tries in controversial circumstances. Billy Warbrick, the Maoris' full-back, began to run with the ball from his own in-goal area after a wayward kick by an England player had almost sent the ball dead. Harry Bedford, one of the England forwards, followed up and put pressure on Warbrick who decided to touch down. As he touched down, Bedford threw himself at the ball and, to the dismay of the visitors, the referee awarded a try to England. Before the interval, Bedford had scored another try in similar circumstances after Harry Lee, one of the Maori forwards, had claimed a touch down after a maul in goal.

The tourists were pretty despondent when they turned round two tries behind at the break, but their annoyance was as nothing compared with the pandemonium that broke out after an England score in the second half.

Andrew Stoddart, one of the English three-quarters (and the last man to captain England at both rugby football and cricket), made a dash along the touchline and seemed set for a try when his shorts were torn in a tackle made by Tom Ellison, one of the Maoris' best players. The players formed the customary guard around Stoddart while he waited for a new pair of pants. In the meantime, the referee allowed play to continue and, to the distress of the tourists, Frank Evershed for England picked up the ball and proceeded to cross unchallenged for a try that John Sutcliffe converted into a goal in his only international rugby appearance. (He was, however, another dual England international who kept goal for Plymouth Argyle, Bolton Wanderers and five times for England.)

Three of the disgusted Native side walked off in protest at this point and for a while the referee allowed the match to continue with England playing against only 12 men. Eventually the New Zealanders' manager persuaded his men to return but England finished comfortable winners.

English rugby had never witnessed such a demonstration as this in an international match and rebukes for the Maoris' reactions were swift in coming. The Union demanded an instant apology from the Maoris. That Rowland Hill, their secretary, had been the referee involved no doubt compounded the insult to the Union over the Maori walk-off.

An apology was forthcoming, but was not deemed adequate enough by the high-minded Union officials, who threatened to effectively cancel the remainder of the tour by forbidding their clubs from playing the tourists. In the end, the tourists had to eat humble pie and Edward McCausland, who had led them in the international, wrote a second apology to Rowland Hill: 'I beg to apologise to the Rugby Union committee for the insults offered by my team to their officials on the field of play on Saturday last.'

The apology had been dictated to the New Zealanders by none other than Hill himself. Nor did the coolness of the Union to the Maoris end there. When the tourists returned to London later in the tour they were socially ignored. Moreover, the tourists received no official send-off when they departed Britain in April.

DÉJÀ VU

MANCHESTER, FEBRUARY 1892

Joseph Jameson must have thought that he was seeing things when he lined up in the Ireland XV to face England at Manchester in February 1892. Either that or he had partaken the night before of one glass too many of the famous whiskey that bore his name. The reason for his confusion was one James Marsh, standing before him in the white jersey and red rose of England. Hadn't this same James Marsh stood before him almost three years earlier at the Ballynafeigh Grounds in Belfast … in the navy blue of Scotland?

Poor Jameson's feelings of déjà vu were not the results of any trickery. This was the very same Marsh whose punting and tackling had played a part in Ireland's downfall by a dropped goal to nil in Belfast in 1889. Marsh, who appeared in the three-quarter line, was a former Edinburgh Institute pupil who qualified in medicine from Edinburgh University.

He won two caps for Scotland before settling in general practice in the Manchester area. As a young man he joined the Swinton club and his strong all-round play came to the attention of the England selectors, who named him as a centre for the annual North versus South match in 1890–1. The following season he won his sole cap helping England to beat Ireland 7–0.

The upshot of his playing for two of the Home Unions is not recorded. Suffice it to say that he is the only man who has ever played for two Unions in the International Championship.

RUGBY VERSUS SOCCER

LONDON, APRIL 1892

Imagine the British Lions taking on the cream of the country's soccer players at a selection of different sports. Jeremy Guscott sprinting 100m against Michael Owen perhaps, Scott Quinnell putting the shot against Paul Gascoigne, or Robert Howley contesting the high jump against David Beckham. And then soccer and rugby games between the teams, before rounding off the event with a limited-overs cricket match involving elevens skippered by Martin Johnson and Alan Shearer.

Far-fetched? Maybe. Yet in 1892 precisely such an unusual sporting challenge featuring the nation's leading footballers and rugby players occurred in a charity festival at Queen's Club in West Kensington.

The protagonists in this pioneering version of Superstars were the Barbarians Rugby Club and the Corinthians Football Club, two sides with such impeccable pedigrees that they were national institutions.

Formed in 1882, the Corinthians were keen to uphold the standards of amateur soccer at a time when the social background of the country's leading footballers was changing. In an earlier incarnation as the Wanderers the team had comprised old boys of the soccer-playing public schools and had won the FA Cup five times. But a tenet of its new constitution prohibited entry to league or cup competition (a rule that was later relaxed). University men and ex-public schools players dominated the club and so gentlemanly were the players that when the Corinthians conceded a penalty their goalkeeper was removed to offer opponents a free shot at goal.

The Barbarians Rugby Club was less exclusive. Founded by an inveterate rugby tourist named Percy Carpmael at an oyster supper in Bradford in 1890, their membership was, in the words of the club's motto: 'for gentlemen in all classes but no bad sportsmen in any class.'

The unique sporting challenge of 1892 was issued by the Corinthians, whose squad included nine players who were or who would become soccer internationals. There were eight established or future rugby caps in the Barbarians' ranks, so it would be fair to conclude that the two codes were pretty well represented when the festival began with an athletics competition followed by a football match on Boat Race Saturday, 9 April.

Despite winning four of the track events the Baa-Baas struggled in the field events, where the matchless talents of one C.B. Fry were displayed. Charles Fry was arguably the best all-round sportsman who ever lived. An athletics, cricket and soccer Blue at Oxford, he would have added a Rugby Blue but for a leg injury. He played soccer and cricket for England and even found time to set the world long jump record.

On this particular day, playing for the Corinthians, he won both the long jump and high jump comfortably to reduce a commanding Barbarians lead and the outcome of the athletics was decided in the Corinthians' favour on the final event, the mile.

Fry then excelled for the Corinthians in the soccer match where the famous Walters brothers, Arthur and Percy, who had played together as full-backs for the England XI, were unperturbed by the unusual tactics of the rugby men. The Barbarians amused the crowd by instinctively resorting to the hand-off as a device for parrying opponents. A hat-trick by Tom Lindley helped the Corinthians to an easy 6–0 win, and after the first day of competition the footballers were two up with two to play.

Surely the Barbarians would resume two days later with a win in the rugby contest? For that match their side would be reinforced by several members of the England pack that a month earlier had completed a Triple Crown of victories in the International Championship without conceding a single score. But they lost. Displaying astonishing ingenuity the dribblers outwitted the handlers. Lindley again showed himself to be a skilful games player, crossing for two tries and impressing the rugby men with his prodigious punting in a 14–12 victory. Newspaper reports of the match suggested that the referee was not fully acquainted with rugby's off-side laws. Even so, the Barbarians were gracious in defeat and many years later one of their committee members recalled, 'the Corinthians were entitled to the glory that follows a fully substantiated challenge.' The rugby players did salvage some respect when the sides met again late in April for the cricket match. Batting first, the Corinthians were dismissed for 170 with C.B. Fry, thinly disguised as 'A. Fryer' on the scorecards, falling for only 25 runs. Australians would consider Fry's wicket cheap at twice that price in several Ashes Tests in later years.

The Barbarians went on to win by four wickets, thanks mainly to an unbeaten 55 from one John Le Fleming, a former England wing three-quarter who was a more than useful performer in the Kent XI. Thus a charming sporting challenge unparalleled in the annals of Britain's two footballing codes ended 3–1 in favour of the soccer players.

WHEN THE CROWD DIDN'T KNOW THE SCORE

CARDIFF, JANUARY 1893

For sheer drama before, during and after a match, the Wales–England encounter of January 1893 took some beating. It was the tenth match of the series and the first that these two sides had played at Cardiff.

The London contingent of the England team travelled down from Paddington on the Friday eve of the match and were unsure whether the game would take place. The south of Britain had been gripped in the jaws of a severe frost for the best part of a month, and the temperature was still well below freezing with snow in the air as the steaming Great Western locomotive pulled into Cardiff station to deliver the England side and accompanying press party.

An eerie, orange hue illuminated the players' short path to their headquarters at the Angel Hotel and the air hung heavy with the smell of burning coal. On their way to the hotel the players passed the Arms Park ground, and one of the pressmen peering through the hoardings compared the sight to a scene from Dante's *Inferno*.

In fact the pitch had become so hard during the prolonged cold spell that the Cardiff groundsman had engaged an army of helpers to keep fire devils (small portable braziers of the type used by street workmen) blazing through the night in an attempt to soften the frosty turf and make it playable for the big match. More than 18 tons of coal were used as workers toiled through the night to thaw the ground.

The plan succeeded, though hundreds of muddy black squares alternated with harder, icy patches to lend the pitch a bizarre chessboard appearance as the two teams emerged early the next afternoon.

Arthur 'Monkey' Gould, the Welsh captain, was the idol of the Welsh sporting public. The outstanding three-quarter of his day, he was also a noted athlete who owed his nickname to his remarkable agility. A dark, handsome man of 28, he had led the Wales XV for four years and was the senior cap in the side. His colleagues had the utmost respect for the Newport man, who had seven of his black-and-amber clubmates with him in the Welsh team.

Andrew Stoddart, the dual international who skippered England at Test cricket and who in 1888 had led the first British rugby touring team to Australia and New Zealand, captained the England side. Winning the toss, he chose to make first use of a biting easterly wind.

The game developed into a titanic tussle between the Welsh backs and English forwards. For seven years before this game the Welsh national side had been committed to playing four three-quarters, a Cardiff club innovation which had never gone down too well with the sizeable Newport contingent that regularly graced Welsh XVs of this time. England in 1893 still preferred to use the orthodox three three-quarter system, and their nine forwards made good use of their one-man advantage to create a couple of tries in the early stages of the match.

At half-time the visitors had what seemed an unassailable seven point lead but, undaunted, Gould spoke optimistically with his men during the interval and gave them inspiration soon after the restart. A Welsh line-out deep inside their own half was the springboard for an exhilarating passing movement which culminated in a try by the captain. Next, a bout of passing by the Welsh three-quarters made an overlap for wing Norman Biggs to dash over in the corner.

That second Welsh try was subsequently viewed as the

ultimate vindication of the four three-quarter system in international rugby. By January 1894, all four of the Home Unions had adopted the formation and never again were nine forwards seen at international level.

The success of the Welsh three-quarters against England, however, was more remarkable for the fact that their left centre, Conway Rees, had been playing with a broken collarbone and could only take and give his passes with one hand. Rees eventually had to withdraw in pain to the touchline and when England's Howard Marshall crossed for his third try (in his one and only Test appearance), Welsh hopes of pulling off a first home victory against England took a dive.

Gould again revived their ambitions with a try from a splendid solo effort that took his side to within a score of England. Then, in the dying moments of the game, Wales were awarded a penalty near the touchline on the England 25. Gould summoned Billy Bancroft, the confident little Swansea full-back, to take a place kick for goal.

An argument appeared to follow. Bancroft, knowing well the hazards associated with place-kicking on a soft and slippery surface, defied his captain and steadied himself (much to the displeasure of Gould) for a drop-kick. The crowd of 20,000 – a record for a Welsh international up to that time – gasped as it saw Gould take offence and turn his back on Bancroft. Undeterred, the full-back let fly with his drop towards the Taff end of the ground, and before the ball had reached the highest point of its trajectory Bancroft turned and shouted to his captain: 'It's there, Arthur.'

Bancroft had kicked the first penalty goal in international rugby and immediately the referee whistled for the end of the game. But what was the final score? Wales finished with a goal from a try, a penalty goal and two tries to England's goal from a try and three tries.

The majority of spectators left under the impression that the result was a 14-all draw, in line with the scoring values then in vogue in Welsh rugby. But in fact the International

Board, the body that laid down the laws for the conduct of international matches, had met only two days before the match and ruled that all goals should be worth three points and tries two. There had been little publicity regarding the change but the mathematics of the matter added up to a 12–11 win for Wales, even though most supporters had left the ground unaware of their side's famous victory.

Wales went on to win the Triple Crown for the first time, penalty goals were to become the bane of international rugby and scoring values were to change several times in the following hundred years as the International Board sought to reward tries above penalty goals.

THE STRANGE DISMISSAL

SYDNEY, JULY 1893

The 1893 New Zealand touring team to Australia played two series of representative matches: one against Queensland and the other against New South Wales during an 11-match tour. Their last match of the visit was the third and deciding match of the rubber with the New South Welshmen. The tourists had won the first game 17–8, but suffered their only defeat of the tour 25–3 in the second match of the series.

They wrapped up the tour in style with a convincing 16–0 victory but there was a curious incident in the second half. The referee, Edward McCausland, was a New Zealander who had settled in Sydney a few years earlier. He stopped play near the end to speak to the New Zealand forward, William McKenzie. McKenzie was the first New Zealander to practise wing-forward tactics and his nefarious activities had earned him the nickname 'Offside Mac'. After a long conversation with the referee he was seen limping towards the touchline where the 20,000 spectators, under the impression that he was retiring injured, with one accord gave him a warm round of applause.

Afterwards the wily McKenzie was rumbled. He hadn't been injured at all: he had actually been sent off and had tried to disguise the fact by feigning injury. He thus became the first man to receive his marching orders while playing for New Zealand.

OXFORD WIN WITH 14 MEN

LONDON, DECEMBER 1900

In the days before substitutes were permitted, the incidence of big matches won by teams depleted through injury was rare. True, Ireland overturned a 0–6 deficit to come back and beat a strong Welsh team in 1904 when they had only 14 fit men on the field for most of the second half. But the game that the old-timers always referred to when discussing results where one team splendidly overcame the odds was the 1900 Varsity match.

The annual battle of the Blues was traditionally held at the Queen's Club in West Kensington at this time. In the lead-up to the match both Universities had compiled similar records so that on the day of the game the betting was described as 'even money'. It was felt that Cambridge had the stronger forwards, while Oxford possessed the more creative back division.

Oxford suffered a cruel blow early in the match when one of their wings, John Crawfurd, an Irish trialist, injured his right shoulder so severely in a tackle that he had to leave the field and played no further part in the game. At first, Oxford refused to withdraw a man from their pack, preferring to risk leaving a position uncovered behind the scrum. With great relief, thanks to some rib-jarring tackling by Jack Crabbie, Oxford reached half-time without having conceded a score.

In the second half, superior Cambridge scrummaging began to take its effect and, helped by two tries scored by their wing, Alfred Hind, they built an 8–0 lead. At this stage, Oxford finally conceded a forward from the pack to cover the gap in the three-quarter line. There followed an amazing swing in the fortunes of the match.

'To have the odds against you [in the Varsity match] is the most inspiring challenge of all,' wrote Howard Marshall of this match many years later when recalling Oxford's rearguard action. First, a well backed up sweeping move took play fully 60 yards (55m) before Ernest Walton raced over for 'one of the finest [tries] in the history of the [Varsity] match'. The try was converted, leaving Cambridge only three points clear.

'This infused fresh life on the contest,' revealed the *Daily Telegraph*, 'and clearly had a disconcerting influence upon the Cambridge men.' Seven minutes from the end, Frank Jones of Cambridge was slow to recover a loose ball and Crabbie was quickly up to sprint away for a try at the posts. The conversion put Oxford 10–8 ahead.

'Even the most phlegmatic spectator could hardly bear to watch,' continued Marshall, until 'after minutes which seemed like hours Mr Harnett's whistle for no-side left Oxford magnificently victorious.' The *Telegraph* concluded: 'Altogether it was a great game, one of the best played between the two Universities.'

A FAMILY AFFAIR

GREYTOWN, JULY 1903

Irish rugby has been noted down the years for the considerable number of brotherly pairs and even trios who have represented the country. The record, however, for most brothers appearing together in a first-class team was first established by the Smiths of Bush in New Zealand.

Five of them took the field for the visiting Bush side in a unique family affair against Wairarapa at Greytown in July 1903. They were full-back George, centre Bill and forwards Gordon, Bob and Campbell. For the record, the quintet were in a 0–16 losing side and never again played together.

They are not well remembered now, even in New Zealand. But conversely, the brothers who equalled the record 58 years later belonged to one of the most famous of all New Zealand rugby-playing clans and are unlikely to be forgotten.

In 1961, the Clarkes of Waikato provided the province with Don (full-back), Doug (centre), Ian (prop), Graeme and Brian (both second-row locks) for the 11–8 win against Thames Valley at Te Aroha. Don and Ian were established All Blacks who, between them, appeared in 55 Tests for New Zealand.

A UNIQUE SCOTTISH TREBLE

JOHANNESBURG, AUGUST 1903

The opening Test of the 1903 British/Irish tour of South Africa at the Wanderers ground provided a unique line-up of captains and referee. The trio were all Scottish internationals. The South African captain was a former Scotland cap, the referee was also an ex-Scotland international, and the leader of the British team was the current Scotland rugby captain.

The tourists' captain, Mark Morrison, was a Scottish farmer who had been first capped as a teenager in 1896. He was still a relative youngster when he took over the leadership of the Scotland side in 1899, and he held the post through 15 internationals up to 1904, to establish a Scottish record that stood unbeaten for more than 70 years. He led Scotland to Triple Crowns in 1901 and 1903.

His opposite number as captain in the South African pack was Alex Frew who, two years earlier, had played under Morrison in the Triple Crown side. Frew was a native of Kilmarnock who qualified as a doctor from Edinburgh University before emigrating to the Transvaal as a young man. Playing alongside him in the Test was another former Scotland forward, Saxon McEwan, who had won 16 caps between 1894 and 1900 and, like Frew, had sought fame and fortune in the Transvaal.

Bill Donaldson, the referee, completed the unique Scottish treble. Donaldson was a former pupil of Loretto School who won Oxford Blues in 1892–4 and later became an iron merchant. A half-back who was one of the first to appreciate the value of tactical kicking, he played six times for Scotland in the 1890s and, in his last international, against Ireland in 1899, he had the distinction of becoming the first Scotsman to score on Scotland's new national ground (at Inverleith, Edinburgh) when he kicked his team's sole penalty goal.

The Test in South Africa appropriately ended in a 10–10 draw, with Alex Frew leading the South Africans by example and scoring one of their two tries. The second Test finished in a scoreless draw, before South Africa took the series with victory in the third. It was the first time that South Africa had won a Test series. They would not lose one at home for another 55 years.

PRIMITIVE TRAVEL ARRANGEMENTS

CORK, FEBRUARY 1905

Modern travel arrangements and the five-star accommodation enjoyed by first-class players today are a far cry from the journey of 1905, when England travelled to Cork to play Ireland in an international at the Mardyke Road ground.

After making a long and uncomfortable boat crossing to Dun Laoghaire, the England team had to endure a gruelling train journey from Dublin across the country to Cork, in which they were 'packed like sardines into a third-class smoker', according to the late E.H.D. Sewell, who was among the press party attending the game. 'Anyone familiar with train journeys in Ireland [in those days] will tell you what that preparation for a match must have been like,' he added.

England were obviously affected by the travelling conditions and Ireland won by the handsome margin of 17–3. To add insult to England's injuries, Basil Maclear, who scored one of Ireland's tries, was a Portsmouth-born Bedford player who had been judged 'not good enough' to play for England by the Rugby Football Union's selectors.

DISBELIEVING SPORTS EDITORS

EXETER, SEPTEMBER 1905

They came, they played, and they almost completely conquered. The original New Zealand All Blacks, the first fully representative overseas Dominion side to undertake a Test tour of Europe, played 33 matches in Britain, Ireland and France in the first half of the 1905–6 season, winning 32 and losing only once.

The tour party arrived in England on 8 September, and made its headquarters at Newton Abbot, where the visitors prepared for their first match of the tour against Devon at Exeter. The only foreknowledge the English press and players had of New Zealand methods was from players who had visited the land of the long black cloud with David Revell 'Darkie' Bedell-Sivright's British team 12 months earlier. Although New Zealand (9–3) and Auckland (13–0) had defeated the British side then, few among the London press corps expected the men in black to succeed on a long, arduous tour in British conditions.

Opinion expressed in the leading British newspapers in the lead-up to the Devon match was that at best the New Zealanders would emerge with honours even. The county were the champions of the South-West (and, indeed, went on to win the English county championship the same season). Views, however, would have to be altered within ten minutes of the kick-off. The tourists simply ran riot. After three minutes James Hunter broke the Devon defence for the first try of the tour. Billy Wallace, who played throughout the match in a sun-hat, converted and then added a penalty. From there on, in the words of the New Zealand manager, George Dixon, 'scores came thick and fast'.

By half-time it was 27–0 and the full-time score was a staggering 55–4. Reporters at the game transmitted the result through to their newspapers ahead of filing their full match reports. When the numbers came in to the various offices preparing their early editions of the Sunday papers, many sports editors were surprised by the score. As winning totals of 50 points were virtually unknown in senior matches at that time, several editors felt there must have been a transmission error and took it upon themselves to 'correct' the scores. One newspaper changed the score to read New Zealand 5, Devon 4 whilst another, acknowledging the strength of Devon rugby, ran with the headline Devon 55, New Zealand 4.

A month later, no such doubts would be expressed. By mid-October the All Blacks had won the first 11 matches of their visit, piling up 408 points and conceding only seven – including just one try. British rugby was beginning to learn its place in the game's global order.

THE REFEREE PERFORMS A SOLO

RICHMOND, NOVEMBER 1905

By the end of October, the All Blacks had played and won 13 matches on the English leg of their tour. Their game with Surrey on the first day of November was remarkable on two counts: for the first time their winning margin was less than a dozen points and the referee was the star of the match.

He awarded 14 penalties against the New Zealanders in the first half alone, and whistled continuously for a procession of minor offences that at first amused but later irritated the crowd. Mr Dixon, the tourists' diplomatic manager, noted: 'From the first, penalty kicks were given with great frequency against New Zealand, generally for infringements in the scrum which, from my position in the stand, were not discoverable.'

More than 10,000 had turned up to see the tourists, about whom the chattering classes were all talking, make only their second appearance in the capital. The referee, it was reported, 'was evidently under the impression that everybody had come to hear him perform on the whistle'.

The *Daily Mail's* critic went to town. Under the banner headline, 'Whistling Fantasia by the Referee,' he proceeded to send up the official at every opportunity. Thus a lady spectator is reported as asking her escort: 'Why aren't the New Zealanders allowed to have a man whistle for them, too?' And when the All Blacks eventually opened the scoring after 25 minutes, with half-back Fred Roberts darting over from a scrum, the report continued, 'When the referee showed signs of fatigue the tourists seized the opportunity to score. The explanation advanced for the referee's lapse was that the pea in his whistle had stuck'.

The pea must have lodged twice more in the second half as New Zealand added two more tries to win 11–0, easily their narrowest margin of victory throughout the English part of the tour. The long-suffering crowd went away whistling and 'instead of the usual rush for the jerseys of the scorers, the crowd made a wild scramble for the referee's whistle at the end'.

The name of this virtuoso? None other than Mr Williams of the Rugby Football Union's committee, the genius who a couple of years later identified for the Union the potential of the market garden site at Twickenham that became known as Billy Williams's Cabbage Patch. Williams was a well-known international referee at this time but, significantly, was not called on to officiate at any of the All Blacks' remaining 20 matches in Europe after his Richmond débâcle.

THE CHIEF CONSTABLE SAVES WALES

CARDIFF, FEBRUARY 1906

Matches between Wales and Scotland invariably settled the International Championship title in the first decade of the twentieth century. A look at the roll of honour for those years will show the reader that the nations exercised a duopoly over international rugby, either Wales or Scotland finishing top of the table every year from 1900 to 1909.

Wales were reigning champions and recent victors over the All Blacks when the nations met for their annual bash in front of 25,000 at Cardiff in 1906. Scotland had been beaten 12–7 by the New Zealanders in a closely contested match but entered the Welsh game full of optimism.

High social status was attached to attendance at Wales's matches at the turn of the century, and even the Chief Constable of Cardiff felt that he should be seen to be on active duty when international rugby matches were played on his patch. On this particular occasion he turned out in his finery as usual, though little did he realise that he was about to play a part in the evolution of the game's laws.

Early in the match, Scotland were pressing. 'Darkie' Bedell-Sivright, a former Lions captain and a strapping wing forward renowned for his dribbling powers, led a Scottish rush into the Welsh 25 and a try seemed certain. He toed the ball over the Welsh line but was astonished to see it strike 'the might and majesty of the stalwart Chief Constable' who was strutting his stuff up and down the Welsh in-goal area.

The Scot reacted quickly, changed direction and managed to touch the ball down to claim a try. But Mr Allen, the Irish referee, ruled 'dead ball' and Scotland's chance of taking the lead was lost. Later in the half, Wales scored tries through Jehoida Hodges and Cliff Pritchard, two of the heroes of their victory over the All Blacks, and finished the match winners by 9–3. Wales went on to retain the International Championship. But the good Chief Constable later warranted his own footnote to the history of the game's laws. The International Board, the body that frames rugby's rules and regulations, subsequently reflected long and hard on the events at Cardiff and introduced a new clause to ensure that any repeat act should be fairly covered.

The outcome of their deliberations was to rule that in future referees should regard all officials and spectators as offending players on the home side, and that any doubt regarding a point or score arising should be awarded against the side responsible for the ground arrangements.

SELECTORS' COCK-UP

LONDON, DECEMBER 1906

One can accept that in the early days of international rugby travelling problems or communication difficulties contributed to teams arriving one or perhaps two short for a big match. But surely the mix-up surrounding the selection of the 1906 England team to face the First Springboks was inexcusable.

One of the prominent forwards of the early part of the 1906–7 season was a Liverpool and Lancashire player named Noel Slocock, who was making a reputation as an effective line-out jumper. The main England trial in those days was the North–South match, and he had already given a tidy account of himself in one of those encounters when the England selectors sat down to deliberate over the XV to meet South Africa at the Crystal Palace in December 1906.

Slocock's name was, by all accounts, put forward for the match but when the team was announced his name was omitted owing to a clerical error. Instead, the name of Arnold Alcock appeared in the team lists. Alcock was a medical student at Guy's Hospital and no more than a useful forward in their Hospitals' Cup side. Yet he was to gain his cap at Slocock's expense.

The student doctor played a part in a creditable 3–3 draw but reports of the match do not single him out for praise. He was never invited to take part in a trial and never again played for England. In later life, however, he was the shining example of the past player who puts something back into the game.

He settled in general practice in Gloucester and from 1924 until 1969 served the club as president. He died in 1973, aged 91, and was the last survivor of his one and only England XV. Noel Slocock scored a try for the Lancashire XV that made the South Africans work hard for victory in their first match after the England Test and, tellingly, came into the England team for their next international. He became a regular member of their pack for two seasons until his playing career ended in 1908, after captaining a losing England side in the Calcutta Cup match. He died young, killed in action in France in 1916.

SEVEN BROTHERS VERSUS SEVEN BROTHERS

CARMARTHEN, APRIL 1909

The credit for devising the seven-a-side version of rugby goes to Ned Haig, a local butcher who arranged the first tournament in Melrose at the end of the 1882–3 season. Within two years there were annual sevens competitions staged at Gala and Hawick and by the turn of the century the abbreviated game had established a unique end-of-season circuit in the Scottish Borders.

Special permission had to be obtained from the Rugby Unions to allow such tournaments to take place and it was not until the 1920s that sevens became a feature of the season in England. Tournaments were long outlawed because they led to the award of prize money, in direct contravention of the laws pertaining to amateurism.

One of the most unusual sevens challenges took place in West Wales at Easter 1909, when a family of seven Williams brothers from Haverfordwest in Pembrokeshire took on the seven Randall brothers of Llanelli. The match was staged on neutral ground at Carmarthen, roughly halfway between the two towns, where more than a thousand of the brothers' travelling supporters turned up to see the 'Family Championship of the United Kingdom'. There was a £100 prize at stake and both sides employed their own trainers to assist with their preparations for a match that was refereed by the ex-Welsh international full-back, Billy Bancroft of Swansea.

The Randalls were brawny steel workers and millmen typical of the working population of Llanelli at the turn of the century. The Haverfordwest boys were sons of the local police superintendent, though none followed their father into the Constabulary. Three were hairdressers, three worked as commission agents and the seventh brother was a clerk.

The match itself was a scrappy, ill-tempered affair according to several local press reports. The Williamses lost one of their brothers through injury early on and Mr Bancroft had to intervene several times as the contest frequently threatened to degenerate into a glorified fight. 'It was more like a wrestling match,' Bancroft commented after the Williamses ran out 8–0 winners.

JOE'S NEW YEAR CAP

SWANSEA, JANUARY 1910

The first ever Five Nations match took place in January 1910 at Swansea, though it is doubtful whether the players who played in the game realised at the time that they were creating a piece of history, by launching what became the jewel in the northern hemisphere's rugby crown. The Five Nations tournament became the byword for European rugby at its best for the rest of the twentieth century.

But back in 1910, the competition came about by accident. France had entered the lists of international rugby on New Year's Day, 1906, with an international against the All Blacks. Later the same year, England crossed the Channel for their first taste of French rugby and two years later Wales hosted the newcomers for the first time. Ireland gave the French an inaugural fixture in 1909 before, the following year, Scotland decided that they, too, would join the *entente cordiale*.

So 1910 is the date from which Five Nations history is reckoned, simply because it was the first time that the round-robin of ten matches involving the nations was completed. The phrase *Tournoi des Cinq Nations* was coined by the French press as early as the 1920s, though its use in the Home Unions did not really catch on until the 1960s.

Could France have made a more inauspicious start to the competition than the events surrounding the departure of their team from Paris for their journey to Wales on New Year's Eve, 1909?

When the players and officials assembled to make their journey to Swansea they discovered that one of their number, a new cap in the forwards named Hélier Tilh, had been forced to withdraw owing to military duties in Bordeaux. The boat train departed with 14 players aboard, leaving one of the French selectors to search the streets of the capital for someone to make up the pack.

At length, the weary official discovered one Joe Anduran working in a picture gallery on the Rue La Boétie. Anduran thought he was the butt of a practical joke when he was first approached about representing his country. Eventually he was persuaded that his services were genuinely required and he enthusiastically joined the selector in a taxi to gather his kit from home.

Preparations for New Year celebrations were well under way back at the Anduran household and poor Joe had plenty of explaining to do to his wife to excuse himself from the forthcoming family festivities. Nevertheless, despite his wife's displeasure, he set off for Swansea and eventually caught up with the rest of the French team on the morning of the match. France were overwhelmed 49–14. The Welsh ran rings around their hapless visitors and raced over for ten tries to two in reply. Poor old Joe didn't even warrant a mention in any of the press reports of the match and he never again received an invitation to represent his country.

Even so, Mme Anduran must have forgiven him for his commitment to the game: in 1913, aged nearly 31, Joe turned out for his club, SCUF (a university sports club in Paris), in the final of the French Championship and collected a loser's medal in a side beaten by Bayonne.

The man who played rugby for his country at the drop of a hat in 1910 was just as quick to serve his country in more serious battles four years later. Joe joined the infantry at the outbreak of the Great War and survived barely two months before losing his life in the fighting south-east of Lens in October 1914. He was 32.

RIOTOUS ASSEMBLY

PARIS, JANUARY 1913

Several of the early international matches staged in Paris were noted for unruly behaviour among the home crowd. Visiting British journalists often ascribed this tendency to a lack of understanding by the French of the game's complex Laws.

Even as late as 1952, incidentally, when France played South Africa at Colombes, the French Federation, anxious to educate spectators, used to print the Laws of the Game on the back of match tickets. Parisians, they realised, were less well immersed in rugby's rules than followers from the south of the country where the game was almost a passion.

One of the worst crowd demonstrations that occurred before the Great War was on New Year's Day, 1913, when Scotland visited the old Parc des Princes to launch that season's Five Nations Championship.

More than 25,000 spectators paid more than 40,000 old French francs to see the Scots win by the comfortable margin of 21–3. Scotland had lost on their only previous visit to Paris and no doubt the big crowd had turned up in anticipation of witnessing another French success.

On the day, though, the strict refereeing interpretations of England's Mr Baxter riled the crowd. Baxter unstintingly applied the letter of the law, usually to France's cost. Scotland scored five tries to one and before the end of the game the partisan crowd wanted blood. It looked as if it would be Mr Baxter's when a faction in the crowd angrily closed in on him as he left the pitch at the end of the match. French officials and players moved quickly to protect him as demonstrating spectators threatened to riot. Not even the presence of mounted police quelled the crowd's antics.

In the end, the quick-thinking of France's wing, Pierre Failliot, saved the day. A former Olympic decathlete and holder of the French 400m record, he came to Baxter's rescue and escorted him at speed to safety behind the stands where a waiting taxi whisked the Englishman off to central Paris.

There was a sad sequel to this match. The Scottish Rugby Union were so disgusted by the reactions of the crowd that they immediately cancelled future fixtures with the French. No match took place between the nations the following season and it was not until 1920 that the series of Scotland-France matches was resumed.

Charles Usher, Scotland's captain in this match, told an amusing story about it in later years. Scotland's full-back in 1913 was Walter Dickson, a South African Rhodes scholar who was deaf. As the Scots walked off among the animated French crowd at the end of the game, Dickson completely misinterpreted the situation and said to his captain: 'It's awfully sporting of them to take their licking like this, isn't it?'

A GAME OF FOUR QUARTERS

WELLINGTON, SEPTEMBER 1913

The weather in windy Wellington, New Zealand, has often led to unusual matches at the city's famous Athletic Park ground. One of the earliest Test matches affected by atrocious conditions was against the touring Wallabies of 1913. The match was the opening Test of a late-season series and was played in a continuous downpour. To make matters worse, a gale force wind caused the wind chill factor to drop below the freezing mark. One newspaper extolled the 5,000 spectators who 'huddling together for warmth and protection from the elements [were] a patient and enduring umbrella and overcoat brigade.'

The referee for the match was Len Simpson, a warehouseman and local official who was in charge of his first Test. Mr Simpson, recognising that the conditions were likely to play a significant part in the run of play, hit on the novel idea of dividing the Test match into four equal periods of 20 minutes, with the sides swapping ends after each break. The players were revived with hot broth during the intervals, with some jumping at the chance to change into dry kit.

The weather became progressively worse as the game wore on and the poor, bedraggled Australians, very much at sea in such foreign conditions, fell further and further behind. New Zealand added three tries in the third and fourth quarters to finish 30–5 winners despite losing their first-choice half-back Henry Taylor, who was replaced at half-time by Frank Mitchinson, a three-quarter.

Len Simpson was a front-line New Zealand referee for a decade and actually accompanied the 1924–5 All Blacks to Britain, Ireland and France as their touch judge. But his unusual move to break a Test match into more than the customary two periods of play is, as far as can be ascertained, unique at international level.

WHERE'S MY SHIRT?

PARIS, JANUARY 1920

The Scottish Rugby Union had a reputation for conservatism and parsimony in the early years of international rugby. They were ardent upholders of the principles of amateurism and refused to meet Wales in 1898 and 1899, alleging that the Welsh Union were supporting professionalism by condoning the launch of a testimonial fund to Arthur Gould, the Welsh captain.

The Scots also harboured other reservations. They had doubts about playing international matches against touring sides and refused to meet the First Wallabies of 1908–9. Therefore, in the 1920s, when the numbering of players was almost universal in international matches, it was no surprise that the Scots were the last to conform. When King George V enquired of the Scottish president at Twickenham in 1924 as to why Scotland were not numbered, back came the reply to HM: 'This is a rugby match, not a cattle market.'

One of the most amusing stories relating to the Scottish Union's tightness was told by Jock Wemyss, who played rugby as a prop forward for Scotland before and after the Great War. Scotland's first international after the Armistice was on New Year's Day 1920 in Paris, on the ground where the riot match of 1913 had been staged. In those days, players brought their own shorts and club socks to international matches, expecting only to receive their jerseys.

Sitting in the changing room at the Parc des Princes before

the match, Wemyss was waiting for his jersey, but otherwise was ready to run out, when one of the Scottish selectors came in to distribute the navy blue shirts complete with thistle emblem. The selector bypassed Wemyss but carried on giving out the jerseys until none was left. At that point, Wemyss enquired about his shirt.

Turning to him, the selector said, 'You played before the war. You were supposed to bring your old shirt.' Despite remonstrating with the baggage man, Wemyss could not convince him that he had no shirt. Even the explanation that he had swapped his jersey with an opponent after his last match (six years earlier) would not wash.

It was only when Wemyss took his place bare-chested in the queue to file out on to the pitch that the Union's official eventually gave in and managed to rustle up a shirt for Jock to wear. Scotland won a hard game played in wet, miserable conditions by a late converted try to nil.

At the final whistle, the referee, England's Frank Potter-Irwin, experienced a fright as the crowd made a bee-line for him. This match was the first between the two nations since the notorious riot game of 1913 when the referee had been nearly lynched by the crowd. Consequently, the French press had issued an appeal to the spectators before the game, asking them to behave politely to the referee and France's Scottish guests.

For a moment, players and officials feared a repeat of the 1913 scenes as spectators closed on Mr Potter-Irwin. But to everyone's relief the enthusiasts' only purpose was to chair him from the ground in a show of sportsmanship that was greeted with applause.

TWO BLIND EYES

PARIS, JANUARY 1922

Rugby players were quick to join up to serve King and Country when, in August 1914, the war to end all wars began. Many clubs saw entire teams enlist and many were devastated by the effects of the war. London Scottish was one of the clubs worst affected. On the last Saturday of the 1914 season the club fielded four senior XVs and all of those involved later joined the Exiles' regiment. Sadly only four returned in 1918 unaffected by their active service. All told, 69 of more than 200 of the club's playing members who served were killed in action. More than 50 were wounded and four were taken as prisoners of war, including Charles Usher who had played international rugby for Scotland in 1914.

Usher survived to lead his country after the war and took part in Scotland's first international of the 1920s, against France in Paris. Three players who appeared in that match had each lost an eye during the war: Scotland's prop, Jock Wemyss, and a couple of Frenchmen including Marcel Lubin-Lebrère who faced Wemyss in the scrums. At the after-match banquet the two struck up a great friendship which was to last for many years.

Arguably one of the most bizarre rugby matches occurred when these two men came up against each other again in the France–Scotland match two years later. Meeting before the match, the two old pals agreed to mark one another in the line-outs.

However, the two rugby Cyclopses had lost different eyes. As a result, in the line-outs along one touchline there was no problem as each was perfectly capable of keeping a beady eye on both the ball and one another. However, once play switched to the other touchline, this was not the case and all hell broke loose as the old veterans barged, shoved and elbowed about, trying to feel their way through the line-outs.

Early in the game the referee's attention was drawn to the two men's blind-side antics. The official was a former England international, Dreadnought Harrison, who was a distinguished recent Services player. Charles Usher, who was now Scotland's captain, was another noted Services player and knew Harrison well.

'What's all this, Charles?' Harrison enquired after first observing Wemyss and Lubin-Lebrère conducting their own game within the game early in the first half. 'Just leave them,' Usher replied. 'It's a private arrangement; they're both half blind.'

Harrison got the message and left them to get on with it for the rest of the afternoon. The battle between the old soldiers was a microcosm of the match itself, the line-out count ending all square on a day when the sides drew 3-all.

TWO FREAK SCORES

TWICKENHAM, JANUARY 1923

Wales made their fifth visit to Twickenham in January 1923. And for the fifth time their journey was made in vain, England winning by a dropped goal and a try to a try: 7–3 under the scoring values then in vogue. This time, Wales could argue that they were particularly unlucky.

Never has a team achieved two such freak scores as England did on this occasion. The first came from the kick-off. A stiff breeze was blowing down the pitch when Wavell Wakefield kicked off into it for England. His kick went straight but, caught in the wind, the ball soared high before falling vertically into the path of Leo Price, the England flanker who was following up. Price ran on towards the Welsh 25 and, seeing his path blocked, took a drop at goal. Again the ball surged into the air, again it fell steeply from its highest point, and again Price was underneath it. This time he had only to canter half-a-dozen yards to touch down to the right of the posts.

England had scored a try ten seconds from the kick-off and before a Welshman had even touched the ball. 'Here was record breaking with a vengeance,' wrote Col Philip Trevor CBE in *The Daily Telegraph*. 'It beat even the famous Adrian Stoop opening to the 1910 game. Much did the multitude indulge in anticipatory joy.'

But the thrill of the first minute did not last. The match settled into a dour struggle between two evenly-matched packs, though, when Wales scored a try six minutes later with the only constructive attacking movement of the match, at least it set up a tight and unpredictable battle. Wales then nearly went ahead when Joe Rees hit the upright with a drop shot, but England were happy to be level at half-time.

The second fluke score, which brought the winning points, came five minutes from time after England, making better use of the wind than the Welsh, had been on the attack for most of the half.

Col Trevor again describes the action: '[Len] Corbett was standing a little in advance of the half-way line and about 20 yards from the touchline when he got hold of the ball. One of the Welsh backs was practically on top of him at the time. He proceeded to do what a stodgy person will prefer to call the lucky, but which I shall take the liberty of calling the clever, thing. He passed the ball obliquely backwards through his legs to [Alastair] Smallwood [who] steadied himself for a fraction of a second and made the long [drop] shot. We seemed to wait an age for the result of the flight of that leisurely ball, but when it did come it was worth waiting for. It was the Tennysonian dénouement. It crossed the bar.'

HONEYMOON SWAN SONG

PARIS, APRIL 1923

Preparations for international matches were certainly different years ago as the following tale involving a former England Grand Slam captain illustrates.

W.J.A. (he was always known as 'Dave') Davies was a Welsh-born outside half who played international rugby for England. His debut for England was in 1913 against the Second Springboks, when he made a favourable impression on the selectors in a 3–9 defeat. For the next ten years he was to remain the outstanding player in his position in England. In a career that brought him 22 caps, he was involved in four England Grand Slams and, after tasting defeat on that maiden appearance against South Africa, he never again featured on a losing England side.

His first season as captain was in 1921 when he steered England to a Grand Slam. The following year he was forced to stand down from the Wales match in Cardiff owing to injury. England lost 28–6 without him, but he returned to lead them unbeaten through the remaining three games of the campaign. The 1923 season was to be his last before retirement from big time rugby. England duly proceeded to defeat Wales, Ireland and Scotland to claim the Triple Crown, leaving the game against France in Paris in April as the Grand Slam decider. Unfortunately, Davies, who was by then a Commander in the Navy, had arranged to marry his fiancée shortly before this game.

He now had to make the decision as to whether he should play in the match or depart on his honeymoon. Davies, however, had no intention of missing the important match and a solution was reached. The happy couple would take their honeymoon in Paris so that the groom could easily get to the Stade Colombes to lead his XV in their important match.

Mrs Davies wholeheartedly supported her husband. She enjoyed sport and was a keen tennis player herself and in later years, even after the death of her husband in 1967, was a knowledgeable rugby follower who regularly attended Twickenham internationals.

THREE PAIRS OF BROTHERS

CARDIFF, MARCH 1924

When Ireland beat Wales at Cardiff in March 1924 they created an unusual record by selecting three pairs of brothers in their XV. The Hewitts, Tom and Frank, were Belfast teenagers who masterminded the victory, each scoring a try. Then there were the Stephensons, George and Harry who were also from Belfast, playing in the three-quarter line, and finally the Collopys, Dick and Billy from the Bective Rangers club in Dublin, who provided brute strength up front.

Frank Hewitt was only 17 and the youngest man to represent Ireland when he made his debut in this match. He sold two dummies on his way to scoring Ireland's third and decisive try in the second half. Earlier, his brother Tom had scored the first and the brothers Stephenson had combined to engineer the second of the scores.

But it was the younger Hewitt who captured the headlines for his performance in this match. 'Still a schoolboy, F.S. Hewitt will be able to look back upon his doings in this match with the utmost degree of personal satisfaction,' reported *Wisden's Rugby Football Almanack*.

BRONZE MEDAL ... JUST FOR TURNING UP

PARIS, MAY 1924

Rugby football was once an Olympic sport. In 1900, France, some six years before their first official cap international, beat Germany and Great Britain. The British team were selected mainly from Birmingham clubs and included only one capped player, a forward named Arthur Darby.

In 1908, Australia took the rugby Gold at the White City Olympics and in 1920, when the sport next featured at the Games, the United States beat France 8–0 in Antwerp. The Americans were bolstered by the presence of Morris Kirksey, one of their track stars who won Gold in the 4x100m relay as well as at rugby, making him one of the rare band who have collected winners' medals at two Olympic sports.

The reigning Olympic champions warmed up for the 1924 competition by playing matches in England where the accuracy and length of their American football-style throws at the line-out impressed opponents. Somewhat surprisingly, the players were not part of the official US Olympic party, but had to pay their own travel expenses and were even held up at Boulogne on the way to Paris by customs officials who queried the validity of their passports.

The Americans opened the defence of their Olympic title against Romania at Stade Colombes, where they experienced little difficulty in overcoming a side that had shipped more than 50 points against the French a week earlier. The American side adopted the New Zealand 5–8 system behind the scrum, but packed down up front in the orthodox 3–2–3 system then familiar to British forwards. Their side was composed almost entirely of students from Stanford University in California and their superior speed and fitness were no match for the Romanians.

Only a tendency to over-elaborate in their handling prevented the Americans from running up more than a 37–0 victory. Frank Hyland in the centre and big Jack Patrick in the forwards were the outstanding players for the States, scoring seven tries between them. The referee was a Welshman named David Leyshon who had settled in France some years earlier.

The US then went on to beat France, who also beat the Romanians. But, despite these two defeats, the Romanians finished with the Bronze medal. Only three nations had entered the rugby tournament: Romania only had to turn up to ensure a medal – and it was the first Olympic honour Romania achieved in any sport.

Unsurprisingly, 1924 was the last year that rugby made an appearance as an official Olympic sport.

THE LAID BACK SAMOANS

APIA, AUGUST 1924

Rugby was brought to the Samoan islands by the Catholic Marist Brothers, but it was not until the arrival of New Zealanders in 1914 that the game was adopted as a national pastime. Until then, primitive matches had been played with empty coconut shells. The expatriates persuaded the New Zealand Rugby Union, whose support of Samoan rugby was a lifeline for more than two decades, to supply the islanders with proper leather balls and by 1924 Western Samoa was ready for its Test debut.

The laid back islanders entertained the touring Fijians in August at Apia. The legend has grown up that the game kicked off at 7.00a.m. to enable the Samoans to get to work and that a large tree was situated on the half-way line. The New Zealand rugby historian, Geoff Miller, who has researched the early days of Samoan Test rugby, confirms that the Samoans launched their international record with a 0–6 defeat by Fiji, but adds that the presence of a tree on the pitch was 'probably a myth'.

Even the reporting of early Test rugby on Western Samoa was pretty casual. Two years after their maiden Test they entertained the Tongans on Apia Park but, according to the Samoa Times of 6 August 1926, its rugby correspondent 'has failed us this week, and owing to a previous engagement at a hopscotch match near the Market Hall on the same afternoon we did not see the Rugby game'.

Nevertheless, despite the absence of a reporter, the newspaper announced that one of its own compositors had been present at the game and that he had reported that Tonga had won 14–5. Their man predicted, 'When Samoa goes down to Tonga next year the footballers of those flat islands will need the biggest tree in Nuku'alofa to hold the notches that will be needed to keep tally of Samoa's tries.' It all seems a long way from the electronic scoreboards of today's modern rugby stadia.

MOMENT THAT SILENCED TWICKENHAM

TWICKENHAM, JANUARY 1925

Like their predecessors of 1905, the All Blacks of 1924–5 arrived for their last international match of the British/Irish leg of their tour looking to preserve their unbeaten record. Between September and December 1924, a side led by Cliff Porter had won 27 matches before, in the New Year of 1925, they wound up their tour with a game against England at Twickenham. In 1905 it was Wales, as the holders of the Home Unions' Triple Crown, who lowered the All Blacks' flag. Twenty years on, it was England's turn as Triple Crown and Grand Slam holders, to offer the last resistance to the tourists.

Until the 1930s, the All Blacks packed down in a diamond formation at the scrums. There were two hookers up front who swung their outside feet inwards to kick rather than heel the put-in back through a scrum that was backed by three second-row men and locked by two men in the back-row. Because the ball whizzed back through the scrum under this arrangement, a scrum-half to put the ball in as well as an eighth man or rover who used to crouch behind the forwards awaiting the heel, were deployed on the fringes.

In Britain the norm was to pack down with three men in the front row: two props supporting a hooker in the middle. Reg Edwards, the Newport prop and captain, had disrupted the All Blacks in their match at Rodney Parade earlier in the tour by taking his front row one step aside as the packs were engaging for scrums, thereby giving his team not one but two loose heads. The New Zealanders, who were going to have none of this, had to take matters into their own hands in order to scrape home against the Welshmen by 13–10.

Edwards was also a seasoned England international (Newport being affiliated to both the English and Welsh Unions) and was chosen for their showdown with the visitors. A record Twickenham attendance of 60,000 packed its stands and terraces on an overcast day. The match, played on a heavy ground, started ferociously with Mr Freethy, the Welsh referee who had also controlled the tour match at Newport, having to sternly lecture both packs for their over-vigorous play. Edwards was again causing the New Zealand front row some problems in the set-scrums and his scrum-capped bald pate was clearly seen at the centre of several exchanges between the packs.

Mr Freethy spoke to the forwards three times in the opening six minutes and warned them that the next transgressor he saw would be dismissed. After ten minutes a line-out degenerated into another fracas and there was a shrill blast of the Welshman's whistle whereupon Cyril Brownlie, one of the New Zealand forwards, was sent off. The crowd fell stunned. Reports say that you could have heard a pin drop as the incredulous crowd watched the crestfallen Brownlie trudge off the field. Embarrassed players – there but for the grace of God went they – fiddled with their kit uneasily as they absorbed the enormity of the occasion. Never before had a player been given his marching orders in an international. And to think it had happened at Twickenham. The Prince of Wales, the future Edward VIII, was a spectator at the match and pleaded in vain at half-time for the New Zealander to be allowed back.

Brownlie's second-row colleagues that afternoon were his brother Maurice and big Read Masters, who later published his diary of the tour. His first-hand description of the event is worth retelling: 'Through the over-keenness of one of England's forwards – who had also adopted illegal tactics in a previous game – heated play was in evidence in the first and many subsequent scrums,' he wrote. 'Thrice the referee issued a general warning to both packs and appealed for calmer play. Then came the climax. After some loose play following a line-out, the whistle sounded, followed by the remark, "You go off."

'Our horror can be imagined when we realised that the remark was directed at Cyril Brownlie,' Masters continued. 'Cyril, without a word, left the field [but] never in my life have I experienced anything like the weird silence that fell over Twickenham as he walked away.'

The teams settled down to play a classic match thereafter. A man short, New Zealand rose to the occasion bravely, their forwards playing like men possessed. Maurice Brownlie, in particular, was a tower of strength in the midst of the depleted All Blacks' pack. With a clear point to make, he scored one of the four tries that helped the New Zealanders build an impressive 17–3 lead. England staged a worthy recovery in the last 20 minutes of the match when the visitors, no doubt exhausted at playing for so long with only 14 men, relaxed. At the end, though, New Zealand emerged with their invincible record intact: England 11, New Zealand 17.

BACK TO SQUARE ONE

TWICKENHAM, JANUARY 1927

Media coverage of international rugby took a giant leap forward in January 1927 when Captain Teddy Wakelam, a former Harlequins player, provided the first live radio commentary of any British sporting event.

The BBC was planning to broaden its scope and keen to adopt the American custom of relaying outside broadcasts of major sporting occasions. Out of the blue, Wakelam was telephoned and asked if he would undergo a microphone test. The former player jumped at the opportunity and within a couple of weeks was perched in a precarious position in the south-west corner of Twickenham, providing commentary on the England–Wales international. The only advice given to him was 'Don't swear.'

A day or two before making his maiden broadcast he had visited the ground with a BBC production team to carry out a reconnaissance, and it was during the discussions that the idea of using a plan of the field divided into eight equal squares was formed. These squares were numbered and as the commentator described the play, his assistant would announce in the background: 'Square three, square two … and back to square one.' The *Radio Times* and Saturday newspapers used to carry the plan of the ground showing the squares, so that those listening at home could follow the game while the commentator was free to concentrate on the names of players and the passages of play.

The experiment was generally well received and the BBC decided to retain Wakelam for the remainder of that season and for many more after it. Rugby was thus brought immediately into the households of those who were unable to attend matches and followers of the game no longer had to rely on newspaper accounts to discover what had happened.

Bernard Darwin, a columnist for *The Times*, reviewed the original broadcast favourably, adding with insight: 'In the course of time all sports and leading outdoor events will be so reported.'

THE FOREGONE CONCLUSION

CARTERTON, AUGUST 1929

Wairarapa began a long series of Ranfurly Shield victories with an 8–7 victory over Canterbury in July 1928. They then successfully defended the Shield through eight challenges before facing Southland at the Carterton Showgrounds on 31 August, 1929. The match was the hundredth of the Shield series, and the holders were so confident of another victory that they didn't even bother to arrange for the Log o' Wood to be brought the 20 or so miles (32.2km) from Masterton, where it was on display in the shop window of Bert Cooke's mercery business. Cooke, the outstanding New Zealand centre of the 1920s and the holders' captain, was one of 11 All Blacks in the side.

By contrast, Southland had only four New Zealand representatives. Moreover, three of their best players failed to arrive in time for the kick-off. But the strong favourites received a jolt in the first 20 minutes as Gil Porter kicked a goal from a mark, a penalty and dropped a goal to put the visitors 10–0 ahead. Wairarapa were stale: they had become a side whose over-confidence was to prove its undoing. Southland led 13–6 at the pause and finished 19–16 – winners with Porter kicking 13 of their points.

It then dawned on the officials that there was no trophy to present. A Wairarapa official was hastily despatched to retrieve the Shield from Bert Cooke's shop so that it could be presented to the new champions.

The whole province of Wairarapa went into mourning and its MP, George Sykes, received a telegram in the New Zealand Parliament which read, 'Deepest sympathies in your sad bereavement.'

After the disappointment of their foregone conclusion, Wairarapa had to wait more than 20 years before briefly holding the Shield again.

LAST-MINUTE TEAM CHANGE

CARDIFF, JANUARY 1930

Sam Tucker of Bristol was the outstanding hooker of the 1920s. He was one of the first Englishmen to specialise in the position, it being common up to the Great War for forwards to pack down in scrum formation simply in the order that they arrived: the so-called First Up, First Down arrangement.

Tucker had already won 22 caps and had helped England to a Grand Slam when, at the start of the 1930 Five Nations Championship, he was dropped from the England side to meet Wales in Cardiff. The England selectors were looking for a fast, fit eight to take on the Welsh and named an experimental pack in which five players were new caps.

On the eve of the match, prop Henry Rew stubbed his toe in training at Penarth. On the morning of the game it transpired that his injury was worse than originally diagnosed and he had to withdraw from the side. Faced with several options, the Rugby Football Union's secretary, Sydney Cooper, telephoned Sam Tucker's Bristol office at 12.25p.m. and, finding the former hooker at his desk, demanded that Tucker get himself to Cardiff pretty damned quick.

Tucker managed to arrange a flight from nearby Filton Aerodrome and, after picking up his kit, took a taxi and boarded a two-seater bi-plane at 1.50. In his own words, Tucker 'was in an open cockpit with what looked to me like a bit of fuselage and a few pieces of wire between me and eternity'. Ten minutes into his maiden flight he was over Cardiff and, after circling around, the pilot landed in a field on the outskirts of the city. Tucker hitched a lift in a coal lorry to the city centre where his next problem was to gain entry to the ground.

A huge crowd had turned up at the gates to see the match. In those days internationals at Cardiff were not all-ticket affairs and it was a matter of first come, first served, as far as admittance to the ground was concerned. Eventually, Tucker managed to talk his way in and arrived in the changing room at 2.40, five minutes before kick-off time. He played hooker with Dave Kendrew, the originally selected hooker, moving to prop. Tucker had a blinder and kept his place in the side for the rest of a season in which England carried off the Five Nations title. For last-minute call-ups Sam Tucker's adventure was unique. But spare a thought for poor Norman Matthews, the Bath and Bridgwater prop who was an England travelling reserve for that Cardiff game. The England selectors, thinking that Tucker had failed to arrange transport, had decided that Matthews would take Henry Rew's place in the front-row. Matthews was actually ready changed into an England jersey when Tucker turned up breathless at the dressing room door.

Matthews never got to wear an England jersey again: a case of so near, so close and so unlucky.

FRENCH OUTCASTS

PARIS, APRIL 1931

For a number of years during the 1920s there had been growing unease in the four Home Unions about the conduct of the game in France. There were suggestions that the intense rivalry of their well organised championship had led to a state whereby several French clubs were being subsidised and controlled in an irregular manner. A number of French clubs were at odds with their own Union and often refused to release players to the national side when big club championship matches were looming.

Matters were brought to a head in early 1931 when a dozen French clubs broke away from their federation to form their own alliance. Such recalcitrance was unacceptable to the Home Unions who, at their meeting of 13 February on the eve of the England-Ireland match at Twickenham, passed a resolution that stated that matches would not be resumed with the French until 'the control and conduct of the game [in France] has been placed on a satisfactory basis'. No slur was meant on the French Federation who, indeed, did all in its power in the months that followed to put the game in France in order. The British felt that there were elements to the split that were reminiscent of the break with England's northern clubs some 40 years earlier, which had led to the formation of the professional Northern Union which later became the Rugby League.

But the timing of the announcement was crass, for the

French were thus given notice of their ejection from the Five Nations championship before they had finished playing all their games in the current tournament. It is hard to imagine the feelings among the two XVs of France and England, let alone the respective committees of the two countries' Rugby Unions, as they convened for the game in Paris on Easter Monday and attended the after-match function.

In its preview of the game *The Times*, understanding the climate in which the match would take place, declared: 'It would be a pity if ill-considered criticisms of British motives incited a holiday crowd to make a demonstration and so upset both teams, who can be relied upon to do their best to improve instead of embitter a rather awkward situation.'

The hopes were largely upheld and in the end rugby football triumphed over politics as the two sides engaged in an exciting match. True, there was a roar of derision when England emerged from their dressing room and the crowd booed them for most of the match. Three times England held the lead before France, through an unexpected drop at goal by Georges Gérald which just scraped over the crossbar, snatched a 14–13 victory. France rejoiced so much at their victory that dark thoughts over being cast out of the Five Nations were temporarily cast aside.

At the after-match function the England captain, Carl (later Sir Carl) Aarvold thanked the French players for a sporting match, revealed that he had always enjoyed playing against them and expressed a wish soon to be doing so again. He was given a standing ovation by his hosts.

The truth was, though, that France had played their last international fixture against a British or Irish XV for nine long years.

THE WRONG SCORE

TWICKENHAM, JANUARY 1933

Wales had already made nine fruitless journeys to the Rugby Football Union's Twickenham headquarters when an experimental side that was a mix of experienced forwards and youthful backs travelled from the Principality to London for the opening match of the 1933 International Championship. Many of Wales's defeats at the ground had been near things and over the years a myth had developed in South Wales that Twickenham was their bogey ground.

High hopes were pinned on a 19-year-old leggy centre from North Wales named Wolf Woollier who was among the seven Welsh newcomers. The teenager enjoyed a successful debut. He was given few opportunities to show his strides in attack but his magnificent side-on tackling, especially in the second half, had the required effect of reducing the danger posed by England's centres.

Even so, England opened the scoring when Don Borland broke through in the first half to send Walter Elliot in for a try. Soon after the interval, however, Wales took the lead when wing three-quarter Ronnie Boon dropped a goal from a loose maul 20 yards (18.3m) from the English posts. That put Wales 4–3 ahead with all to play for. The Welsh pack began to exercise a hold on their opponents, though only Wooller's tackle at the corner flag prevented Elliot from restoring England's lead after a 30-yard (27.4-m) chase.

Then Ronnie Boon put Wales further ahead with a try

that was followed by a most unusual incident. Welsh centre Claude Davey drew the English full-back perfectly to release Boon on a run that took the wing arcing outside the defence for a try near the posts. Viv Jenkins, making his Welsh debut despite nursing a high fever, lined up the simple kick and sent the ball, so the Welsh supporters and Welsh touch judge thought, straight between the posts. Even the scoreboard operator believed that the kick was good, for he marked up a Welsh lead of 9–3 with time running out. Converted tries were worth only five points at this time, so most of the crowd and probably the players, too, felt that Wales were virtually safe with England having to score twice to win.

That, however, was not so. Only at the end of the match was it made clear by the Irish referee, Tom Bell, that Jenkins's conversion kick from close range had failed. It was true that Mr Llewellyn, the Welsh touch judge, had signalled a goal. He was from Bridgend, Jenkins's home club, and presumably could not believe that the young place kicker would miss a kick from such a good position.

The score had come ten minutes from no-side and the misunderstanding could have had a profound influence on the outcome of the match. The fact was that England only needed another breakaway try and conversion to win the match. Whether or not the English players were aware of the position is not recorded, though it was reported that the Welsh forwards so dominated the closing stages of the match that it was as much as England could do to prevent Wales from increasing their lead.

A similar incident in the Paris international between France and Scotland in 1951 might have had more serious consequences. A French conversion attempt on the stroke of half-time was touched in flight by a Scotsman and therefore disallowed by the referee. But the Stade Colombes scoreboard operator, Jacques Robin, credited his side with the two points after an announcer had given the score as 8–6 to France instead of 6–6.

The second half was a see-saw affair and with five minutes remaining Scotland actually led 12–11 while the scoreboard showed France ahead 13–12. The referee was the well-known English official Tom Pearce, who had earlier communicated the correct score to the marker in the score box. The 30-year-old Monsieur Robin, however, deliberately ignored requests to change the scores, despite pleas from the French officials as well as from the referee.

'I was afraid of trouble from the crowd if I corrected the scoreboard,' he told reporters later. 'I was waiting for the loudspeaker to announce the correction, but it remained silent,' he added.

Fortunately a major incident was avoided when Jean Prat landed what turned out to be France's winning points from a penalty goal only three minutes from time. British journalists attending the match were unanimous in siding with the score-marker's view, noting that the French crowd was the most partisan seen since the war.

THE FULL-BACK WHO FLOUTED CONVENTION

SWANSEA, MARCH 1934

The introduction in 1968–9 of the so-called Australian dispensation law which restricted direct kicking into touch to within the defending side's 25 had far-reaching effects. International matches were opened up and the role of the full-back, formerly the last line of defence, radically changed. Full-backs became attacking weapons and tries scored by number 15s increased like the proverbial mustard seed in the following years.

But for the first half of the twentieth century, the job description of the full-back was to tackle, catch safely and kick to touch. Then, in 1934, one player showed the way ahead by flouting convention to become the first from his position to score a try in the International Championship.

His name was Vivian Jenkins of Bridgend. He had learned the game at Llandovery College before going up to Oxford University, where he won three Blues as a strong attacking centre between 1930 and 1932. He had been expected to enter the Welsh side of 1933 in his Varsity position but had converted to full-back at the behest of the Welsh selectors for the final trial that season. He was to become the outstanding player in Britain in his position during the 1930s.

The match with Ireland at Swansea in 1934 had been running for more than hour before Jenkins's moment of history arrived. The Irish, who had had the better of the match, twice came within an ace of scoring in the first half but, as the game entered its final ten minutes, the teams remained deadlocked.

An Irish kick deep into Welsh territory was fielded on his own 25 by Jenkins, who initiated an attack. Showing the skills that made him such an effective centre at Oxford he gained 30 yards (27.4m) before passing to Idwal Rees the Welsh right centre. Rees took play into the Irish 25 where, faced by the defending full-back, he passed out to Arthur Bassett, his wing. The cover managed to race across, but as Bassett was smothered into touch he released the ball in-field where Jenkins, who had followed up instinctively behind his three-quarters, was at hand to pick up and calmly cross for a try which he converted from a wide angle. Wales scored twice more in the next five minutes to finish winners by the rather flattering margin of 13–0.

The Welsh full-back's action caused an outcry among some sections of the rugby fraternity. The purists argued that it was not the done thing for a full-back to score a try, especially in an international. Instead, they claimed, Jenkins should have followed the coaching manual and booted the ball into touch when he first received it. Suffice it to say that no full-back scored a try in the Championship again until 1962.

ALL BLACKS BEATEN BY SCHOOLBOYS

SWANSEA, SEPTEMBER 1935

Official New Zealand teams had played 67 matches on European soil and lost just once (to Wales by a try to nil in 1905) when the Third All Blacks of 1935 arrived at Swansea to play the All Whites in the fifth match of their tour.

The day was one that west Wales folk are familiar with, a persistent drizzle coming in off the sea from mid-afternoon until dusk. These were conditions which Old Stager, Welsh rugby's leading critic of the day, had referred to whilst staring into his crystal ball when preparing his morning of the match preview: 'With heavy going and a greasy ball the tourists may be less convincing. Our visitors may meet with an unpleasant surprise if they run against one of the best Welsh sides [Swansea] in foul weather.'

But the weather wasn't the only factor that would surprise the All Blacks. Swansea's half-backs were Willie Davies and Haydn Tanner, Gowerton cousins who had been the pivotal point of a successful All Whites' XV since the previous September. These two were in the best Welsh half-back traditions: quick-witted, sure of foot and brilliant individualists who could also function intelligently as part of the team. Neither had yet played for Wales, but within the space of six months both would win their caps.

The cousins revealed sound tactical judgement from early on in the match, playing with sureness and at the same time weighing up their famous opponents. Their constant probing runs worried the All Blacks and gave confidence to a Swansea pack that soon began to hold its own up front.

It was from a forward drive that Swansea opened the scoring. The New Zealanders were forced to concede a line-out and from the throw-in Dennis Hunt scrambled over. Thereafter the match was always thrilling and contained many movements which, in the words of another Welsh correspondent, 'permitted real rugby lovers to drink deeply of the champagne of the game'. The first glass of bubbly was a Swansea vintage. Willie Davies, who was varying his game cleverly, completely tricked the visitors' defence with a jinking run and opened a huge gap for Claud Davey to stride 30 yards (27.4m) unchallenged for a try that Wilf Harris converted.

New Zealand pulled back three points with a Nelson Ball try, but before half-time the Swansea halves had engineered another score. Davies again sent the New Zealand defence the wrong way and once again Davey was the beneficiary, bringing the score to 11–3 at the interval.

It was then that the weather set in and, during a second half that produced no further scoring, the Swansea forwards, matching the bigger New Zealanders in the heavy conditions, made victory possible. But it was the halves who had made it certain, as the tourists' captain, Jack Manchester, acknowledged at the after-match reception.

'Haydn Tanner and Willie Davies gave a wonderful performance,' he said, 'but please don't tell them back home in New Zealand that we were beaten by a pair of schoolboys.'

Indeed, Tanner and Davies were schoolboys, both being in their last term at Gowerton County School at the time of this first ever defeat of New Zealand by a British club side.

FIRE BRIGADE HOSES CROWD

CARDIFF, MARCH 1936

The 1936 Wales-Ireland match was quite simply the game everyone wanted to see. Unbeaten Ireland were seeking their first Triple Crown since 1899, while Wales, who had earlier in the season beaten the All Blacks by a point, could win the International Championship by beating the Irish.

The whole of Wales and most of Ireland descended on Cardiff on Saturday 14 March to witness the match of the season. Internationals were not all-ticket affairs in those days and the crowds admitted to many rugby grounds for championship deciders or tour matches would make modern day officials with responsibility for crowd safety wince in disbelief. At many matches spectators were put under severe stress by the crushes created from overcrowding on the terraces. However, never before (nor indeed since) had the authorities taken matters into their hands to the extent that the Cardiff Fire Brigade did on this early spring day.

Long before the 3.30 kick-off the ground was full. Queues had formed in Westgate Street at breakfast time even though the gates did not open until 11.30a.m. By 1.00p.m., two and a half hours before the kick-off, the gates were closed. Some of the huge crowds locked out, however, burst through a police cordon at one of the ground's main entrances and thousands poured on to the terraces.

Later, a further and potentially more dangerous influx of people onto the terraces was prevented by the actions of the Cardiff Fire Brigade. A boat train of Irish supporters had arrived from Fishguard after the Westgate Street entrance had been shut and, on finding they were not going to be allowed into the ground, the angry late arrivals began scaling the gates to get in. It was then that the Cardiff Fire Brigade sprang into action, turning their hoses on the miscreants to deter them. The measure was successful and the invaders withdrew, their spirits suitably dampened, and a major disaster was probably averted.

Even so, when the match began, more than 70,000 were estimated to be present. The crush was so intense that a 60-year-old man from Trealaw near Pontypridd collapsed and died in the ground, a Newport man was detained in hospital suffering from concussion, 18 received minor injuries and the St John's Ambulancemen were kept busy during the match as more than 200 walking wounded sought attention.

Under these conditions, the patience of the players and of the referee, Mr Cyril Gadney of England, were severely tested before the match could be completed. Sensing the danger to lives from the huge crushes on the terraces, policemen helped those who were pinned to the enclosure fencing onto the field. The move prompted a surge of other spectators to jump over and crowd the touch lines and goal lines. As a result, when play settled at the west end of the ground, those packed behind the east goal trespassed infield, and vice versa.

On several occasions the match had to be interrupted for spectators to be cleared from the field of play. Photographs of the match show the Welsh touch judge, Lot Thorn of Penarth, having to patrol his line from inside the field of play as spectators more than a dozen deep lapped over from the old north enclosure. Players throwing in to line-outs were handed the ball by supporters standing literally at their elbows. It was a tribute to the teams and Mr Gadney that the game was completed.

The match itself was an exciting one in which no quarter was asked and none given. The Welsh forwards played above themselves, surprising the visiting Irish pack who were expected to carry all before them. The conditions were ideal for running rugby, but the tension of the occasion dictated that tactics should be kept tight and the only score of the match was a penalty goal kicked by Viv Jenkins for Wales in the twentieth minute of the first half.

WARTIME CAPS IN PARIS

PARIS, FEBRUARY 1940

The 1939–40 rugby season promised to be the most significant one of the decade. A full-scale tour of Britain by the Wallabies was scheduled to start in September and, with playing relations renewed with France, a full Five Nations championship was on the cards for the first time for nine years. All told, 15 full international matches were due to be played that winter.

The outbreak of war on the first weekend of the season meant goodbye to all that. On arrival, the Australian tourists spent a week on the south coast packing sand-bags before joining up, while the Home Unions promptly cancelled all fixtures for the season. Clubs were eventually permitted to arrange games if they were prepared to comply with government war-time regulations and an interesting informal season followed while Britain waited uneasily during a period of Phoney War.

However, an Army XV full of international players took part in a highly entertaining match at the Parc des Princes against France in February of that season. The French, delighted at their return to international competition, awarded full international caps to their players. By doing so they made the match unique in the game's history, for it stands as the only major official international ever staged on a continent at war.

The Army XV, which defeated the French 36–3, was a high-powered side. Its players read like a cavalcade of British Rugby stars of the 1930s: Viv Jenkins, Peter Cranmer, Wilf Wooller, Sammy Walker, Mike Sayers, Blair Mayne and Bill Travers. All were among the top players of their generation and most of them had toured South Africa with Walker's 1938 Lions. Many reckoned the team to be one of the best British sides ever. Wooller was outstanding, scoring a hat trick of spectacular tries and Jenkins kicked seven conversions.

The only other major Test staged during wartime was in August 1914 when the All Blacks and Wallabies played the third international of a New Zealand tour to Australia. The match in Sydney took place shortly after the Great War broke out in Europe.

END OF THE ROAD

TEDDINGTON, JANUARY 1945

Which was the most successful club side ever? It's an impossible question to answer but nonetheless one that is debated endlessly in any number of pubs and clubs. The Oxford University side of the 1880s enjoyed a long unbeaten run in the early days of the game, and Harlequins enjoyed a successful spell in the years leading up to the outbreak of the Great War at about the same time as they moved to Twickenham.

Then there were the Northampton teams of the 1950s, who for more than a decade had at least one representative in every England Test side, while in the more recent era of the Cup and Leagues, Bath's records take some beating. But the common ground shared by such successful sides is that, whenever they were beaten, there was always genuine surprise among the spectators that the favourites had been overcome.

The end of what must be the longest run of victories by a club side was witnessed by a similarly dumbfounded crowd at Teddington in January 1945 when a young St Mary's Hospital XV, with an exciting midfield triangle, brought to an end the golden run of Coventry in a tense match. It was the medics' Nim Hall, later a distinguished utility back for England, who was the architect of the home side's win. The fly-half dropped both of his side's goals (worth four points apiece then) in an 8–3 win against the Midlanders.

The result marked the end of a truly incredible run of 72 victories by the Coventry club which dated back to December 1941. In that time they had amassed 1712 points and conceded only 254. That they should lose to a team of student doctors added to the surprise of the thousand or so spectators who were present at the match. For the record, Coventry beat the medics 14–0 in a return match at Coundon Road a couple of weeks later.

PASSPORT SCAM

PARIS, APRIL 1946

After the wartime break, responsibility for arranging international matches returned to the Home Unions in 1945 and for the season 1945–6 an informal series of representative matches was staged. Additional interest was provided by the Kiwis, a team of New Zealand Services players who engaged in internationals with England, Scotland, Wales and France, although no caps were awarded by the British or Irish unions. With many British servicemen still abroad, it was argued by the Home Unions that their international sides were not truly representative. The French, however, recognised all of their matches as full cap games.

The public, untroubled by the issue of caps or not, flocked in their thousands to see a series of matches that became known as the 'Victory Internationals'. There was no championship at stake, because it was impossible to arrange a complete round-robin of fixtures but this did not detract from the allure of the fixtures.

The last international of the series was staged at Stade Colombes where Wales were the visitors but, due to last minute changes, the party travelling to Paris for the match had to deceive Customs in order to field a full XV.

Cliff Davies, the Kenfig Hill miner who was one of the most popular Welsh players of his generation, was supposed to prop for Wales on this occasion. When he was injured in a colliery accident shortly before the party was due to set off for France, his cousin, Billy Jones, was hurriedly drafted into the side despite suffering a painful ear injury playing for Cardiff against the Barbarians on the eve of departure.

There was, however, a problem. Billy Jones had never been abroad and didn't possess a passport. Fortunately, for the Welsh party, he bore a strong resemblance to his cousin and this presented a way round the problem. Billy simply travelled under Cliff Davies's name and carried his cousin's papers. And he got away with it. All the match reports of the game reported the name C. Davies (Cardiff) in the team line-ups for the game. One critic at the match even referred to 'Cliff Davies's fine play', which must have tickled the two cousins pink.

Whether the Welsh Rugby Union enlightened the press and asked for confidentiality about the change is unknown, but certainly everyone in the cousins' home village of Kenfig Hill, where both of them were local heroes, knew the secret of the Welsh front-row in that last international of the 'Victory' season.

For the record, France won by 12–0, their halves successfully blotting out the threat posed by the Cardiff pair of Billy Cleaver and Haydn Tanner.

THE ALL BLACK DAY

WELLINGTON AND DURBAN, SEPTEMBER 1949

Saturday 3 September, 1949 was a unique day in the history of international rugby. For the only time since Tests began in March 1871, a country fielded two separate XVs on the same day for cap matches.

The country in question was New Zealand and the games took place on two different continents. The day began in Wellington where virtually the third New Zealand XV faced Australia in the opening match of a two-match series. The Wallabies, led by Trevor Allan, played effective rugby and scored three tries in the 20 minutes leading up to the interval to lead 11–0.

New Zealand came back after the break. Jack Kelly landed an eighth minute penalty before Graham Moore, on his only appearance in an All Black shirt, scored a try. But Australia's determined defence held up and at full time the score was 11–6 to the Wallabies, who thus registered their first success against New Zealand for 15 years.

Later the same day, across the Indian Ocean in South Africa where New Zealand's leading 30 players were simultaneously making a major tour, the All Blacks played the third match of their Test series in Durban. They had already lost the first two matches of the series and for this game their tour skipper, Fred Allen, had been dropped. Bad enough as these events were for New Zealand rugby fans, for those who listened in late at night to the radio commentary of the events of that match there was even more depressing news to swallow. After a promising first half the tourists eventually went down 9–3, thus losing their third consecutive Test in South Africa and with it the chance of squaring the series.

This sequence of losing Test matches was extended to six by the end of the 1949 season as New Zealand went on to lose the Fourth Test in South Africa and the second Test against Australia. Never before and never since have the All Blacks lost six Tests on the trot and, if 1949 has gone down in their rugby annals as the Black Year, then Saturday 3 September, 1949 was certainly their Black Day.

FATHER VERSUS SON

GISBORNE, SEPTEMBER 1950

The first time that a father and son faced one another in a first-class match in New Zealand was in September 1950. George Nepia senior, golden boy of the 1924–5 Invincible Second All Blacks who toured Britain and France, was 45 years of age when he turned out at full-back for the Olympians invitation club against Poverty Bay in Gisborne.

Opposite him, also as full-back, was his son, George Nepia junior. Both players were captains of their sides on a day when age triumphed over youth. The Olympians won 17–11, the victorious captain setting another record on that occasion by becoming the oldest New Zealander to feature in a first-class match.

MURRAYFIELD MASSACRE

EDINBURGH, FEBRUARY 1951

Scotland won a rare and famous victory that is still discussed when old men gather to talk about the Five Nations championship. Wales, the reigning Grand Slam champions, started their match against virtual no-hopers, Scotland, at a cracking pace in front of a then world record attendance of 80,000 spectators, nearly a quarter of whom were Welsh. They tore into the Scots and immediately put them on the defensive.

Twelve of the Welsh XV had toured Australia and New Zealand with the Lions several months earlier, but Scotland showed that they were no great respecters of reputations and safely survived the initial Welsh onslaught. Scotland's loose trio effectively disrupted the Welsh halves and fly-half Glyn Davies was so harassed out of the game that towards the end of the match the Welsh captain, John Gwilliam, in desperation rearranged his midfield and switched Lewis Jones from centre to the pivot position.

The Scottish back row in fact had set the agenda almost from the start of the match. At the first scrum, Wales heeled the ball and Rex Willis threw out a routine pass to Davies, his half-back partner. The Scottish flankers, Doug Elliot and Bob Taylor, were on him like hawks and poor Davies was buried beneath a wave of marauding blue jerseys. Aggressive defence was to be the key to Scotland's growing threat. As the first half progressed, Scotland gained the upper hand up front and it hardly surprised the experts when the Scots reached half-time nursing a slender 3–0 lead, their full-back Ian Thomson having kicked a penalty goal.

The third quarter of the match was uneventful until Peter Kininmonth, the Scottish captain, inspired his side with an unexpected score. Welsh full-back Gerwyn Williams missed touch with a kick from inside his own 25. Kininmonth caught the ball near the touchline, lined the goal up in his sights and sent a lovely drop goal spiralling between the posts.

Thereafter the Scottish backs played sound rugby football to score three tries against a Welsh defence that fell to pieces. New cap Robert Gordon crossed twice, supporting a break by Donald Scott for the first try and diving on a loose ball after a rush led by Doug Elliot for his second. Jim Dawson, a forward, completed the rout of the Welshmen, scoring seconds from time when he picked up in the loose and charged over.

Scotland's famous massacre of Wales – wins by 19–0 were very rare in the early post war era – stands as the most remarkable 'David and Goliath' match in Five Nations history. 'This was one of the most extraordinary results I can remember,' began Dai Gent in his *Sunday Times* report of the match. Gent, never one to overstate the case, had played international rugby as far back as 1905 and, in a long and distinguished career in journalism, was one of the game's most knowledgeable and respected critics.

Many explanations were offered for what amounted to an incredible change in Welsh form: the more plausible were that too many of their players were stale after the long Lions tour and that the team were complacent after giving England a 23–5 hiding only a fortnight earlier.

Yet the truth of the matter was that Scotland were the more enthusiastic side and wanted the win more than the Welsh did. The spirited Scots thoroughly deserved their great triumph but, had they known what lay in store for them, they would gladly have settled for a less spectacular win in return for more victories. For before the year was out the Scots were involved in another Murrayfield massacre when they were on the receiving end of a 44–0 thrashing by the touring Springboks. And four more years (and 17 successive Tests) would pass before Scotland again won an international match.

DID THE TOUCH JUDGE HELP WALES?

CARDIFF, DECEMBER 1953

Until 1963 Wales had never lost to the All Blacks at Cardiff. It is incredible to reflect today that their wins there in 1905, 1935 and 1953 once gave them a 3–1 lead in this series (they lost at Swansea in 1924). Even so, there was never more than one score between the sides in the matches won by Wales.

Probably the luckiest Welsh win of the three was in 1953 when they beat New Zealand for the last time. It was 8–5 to New Zealand as the game entered its last quarter. Welsh three-quarter Gareth Griffiths had gone off with a badly dislocated shoulder in the first half, but pleaded with the Welsh Rugby Union's surgeon, Nathan Rocyn-Jones, to allow him to return to the match. After Griffiths returned, Wales redoubled their efforts, and managed to kick a penalty goal that levelled the scores. Five minutes from time Griffiths was to figure in the move that led to the winning score.

He and left wing Gwyn Rowlands put pressure on New Zealand's Allan Elsom, some 20 yards (18.3m) from the All Blacks line. As the ball went loose, Clem Thomas picked it up and, finding himself cornered close to the touchline, cross kicked. The ball bounced into the path of the Welsh right wing, Ken Jones, who raced over for a try at the posts, which Rowlands converted. 13–8 to Wales and that was that.

It was another Welsh winner against New Zealand, Viv Jenkins of the 1935 side, who later spun an intriguing tale around that winning move. He became a leading post-war rugby journalist, first with the *News of the World* and later for *The Sunday Times*. Jenkins attended the dinner after the 1953 match and was seated beside another former Welsh great, Ifor Jones of Llanelli, who regularly acted as Wales's touch judge during the 1950s. Jones had been running the line that afternoon, and discussing the day's game, Jones divulged to Jenkins that as Clem Thomas picked up the ball, he had yelled, 'Cross-kick, Clem; Ken Jones is unmarked.' Did a touch judge really help Wales to beat the All Blacks?

Although referees were neutral, those were the days when each of the sides playing provided their own touch judge for international matches. Usually these were members of the participating Unions' committees or distinguished referees. More than 30 years were to pass before neutral touch judges arrived on the international match scene.

Ifor Jones and Clem Thomas, sadly both dead now, were great characters and wonderful story tellers. The truth of the tale has never been proved. But certainly the film of that winning move shows the Welsh touch judge right up with the play at the time of Thomas's cross-kick. Ifor Jones was unquestionably in the ideal position to influence the kicker. Clem Thomas, moreover, was described as looking pale and worried during the match, weighed down no doubt by the distress of having been involved in a fatal road accident on his journey down to Cardiff on the eve of the game.

It is easy to believe that Clem was operating on auto-pilot for once in a distinguished rugby career that culminated in his captaincy of Wales in nine matches in 1958 and 1959, and that he was quite happy to follow the inspired instructions of 'his' touch judge. But many of Clem's friends on hearing this story years later insisted that the tale was more likely to be the product of Ifor Jones's fertile imagination.

Clem was a well-known rugby journalist up to the time of his death. His former Press Box colleagues, categorically dismiss the story: 'Can't be true', they say almost to a man. 'Clem would never have done as he was told.'

THE OVERBEARING CAPTAIN

TWICKENHAM, FEBRUARY 1955

Jean Prat was the outstanding French rugby player of his generation. He was a regular fixture in the Tricolores' XV from 1945 until his retirement from internationals in 1955 and did much to raise the profile of French club rugby in immediate post-war seasons. At his own beloved Lourdes he fittingly performed miracles, raising the small town club to champions of France.

Determination and tenacity, legacies of his prowess as a long-distance runner, were the distinguishing features of his own game and when, in 1953, the captaincy of the French side fell vacant he was seen as the natural choice to lead the side. Within 12 months he had taken France to the top of the Five Nations Championship for their first ever title.

He had at his disposal a very young side in 1954 and led with an iron fist. Instigating a tight-marking policy he carried his men to wins against Scotland, Ireland, New Zealand and England, though a narrow defeat against Wales in Cardiff meant that France's maiden Five Nations title had to be shared.

The 1955 season, he had decided, would be his last in international colours and Monsieur Rugby, as he was called on both sides of the Channel, decided that he wanted an all-out commitment from a team that he was determined to lead to the Grand Slam. Wins against Scotland and Ireland took his unbeaten men to a difficult contest with England at Twickenham on the last Saturday of February.

The match at rugby's Mecca was a tight one and Prat gave one of his best individual performances. He so dominated the proceedings that even his own team were in awe of him. Amédée Domenech, then a callow prop, found his captain's exhortations to do this, do that and do everything so overbearing that at one point, finding himself unexpectedly in possession, he determined to put his captain in a likewise situation. He passed the ball like a hot potato to Prat. But before Domenech could mutter, 'Here, see what you can do with it,' the captain had dropped his second goal of the match and set his side on course for a 16–9 win – only their second success since 1911 at Twickenham. Domenech was dumbfounded.

ENTIRE WELSH XV ORDERED OFF

CARDIFF, MARCH 1957

International matches at Cardiff in the late 1950s and early 1960s were invariably mud-baths. The history of the ground until its redevelopment as the National Stadium in 1969 was closely associated with famous Welsh matches played on what one critic described as far back as the 1920s as their own 'primordial slime'.

Many people will have fond memories of being drenched on the old, open East or West terraces at the Arms Park. In March 1957, Wales hosted Ireland on a typical South Wales day. The rain had been falling in stair-rods from a slate grey sky since dawn when the sides squelched their way across the turf and lined up for the start of a match that odds-on would depend on weight advantage.

But on this occasion the conditions were so bad that the referee was prompted to take action that was subsequently outlawed by the game's rule makers, the International Board.

Wales took the lead after eight minutes when Terry Davies kicked a penalty goal from a wide angle after Ireland had infringed at a line-out. The ball was still relatively new and light at this stage, which could not be said ten minutes later when Ireland missed the first of three attempts to equalise from positions that would have been considered easy in different weather.

Passing and running were becoming increasingly difficult

as the pitch turned into a quagmire and it was to their considerable credit that Ireland managed to fashion a try midway through the first half. The conditions were entirely to blame for a Welsh lapse.

Cliff Morgan was caught in possession and sent a pass backwards to Terry Davies, his full-back. Davies lost his footing and as he fell the slippery ball spilled loose, whereupon back-row forward Ronnie Kavanagh dived on it to claim a try that, from close range, Cecil Pedlow converted to give Ireland the lead.

Play in the second half became a lottery. The heavier Welsh forwards, however, began to take charge of the set-pieces, though no-one looked capable in the difficult conditions of holding the ball long enough to create a try.

On the hour the referee blew loudly on his whistle and began talking earnestly to both captains. At length the entire Welsh XV left the field with the apparent blessing of the referee. The 30 players had become so camouflaged by the mud that it had become impossible for the official to tell the teams apart, so he had offered both teams the opportunity of changing into clean shirts.

Only the Welsh took up his offer. The Irish preferred to stay on the field in the wet and cold, running on the spot while the Welsh retreated to the warm, dry dressing rooms. Undoubtedly Ireland erred in their decision. For when the Welsh returned they were noticeably uplifted by the change of kit and ten minutes later forced a penalty from which Terry Davies, at point blank range, was able to lift the heavy ball over the crossbar for the winning points.

The referee making his international debut on this occasion was the Scottish official, Jack Taylor. A former Leicester fly-half, Jack was for many years a master at the famous Scottish school, Loretto. His unusual action in offering the teams the chance to go off was not appreciated by the International Board. He was not invited to officiate at an international match for three years and when the game's law books were amended for the 1957–8 season, a clause prohibiting teams to leave the field at any time between kick-off and no-side was inserted.

Mr Taylor did eventually return to Wales on international duty in 1960 for the Wales–South Africa clash. Unfortunately for him the conditions then were even worse than they had been for the Irish match. (The morning after the South Africa clash the river Taff burst its banks and flooded the Arms Park). During the match the pitch turned into such a morass that the touch- and goal-lines became completely obliterated. There were also frequent stoppages while players had to use towels to remove mud from their eyes.

Unable to interrupt the match this time, either for the players to change or for the groundsman to repaint the markings, Mr Taylor simply offered to abandon the game after 55 minutes. But his offer was turned down. Terry Davies, Wales's captain, steadfastly refused, believing that his side could win as they were trailing by only three points and had the gale behind their backs. South Africa, however, somehow managed to hold on to win in conditions to which they were 'loathsomely unaccustomed'.

Certainly, Jack Taylor never forgot his refereeing experiences at Cardiff.

THREE REFEREES FOR ONE MATCH

PAHIATUA, SEPTEMBER 1957

The game between Bush and Wanganui played at Rugby Park, Pahiatua, near the end of the New Zealand domestic season in 1957 was unique for the fact that three referees were used in a first-class match.

The official who started the game was Roy Rice. He was then injured in a collision with a player scoring a try and had to withdraw to the touchline for treatment. As preparations for the conversion kick were being made, Leith Parker, one of the match-day touch judges who was also the president of the Bush Union, stepped in to supervise the kick and awarded the points for the successful conversion.

When it became apparent that Mr Rice would be unable to complete the match, a third referee, Wray Hewitt, officiated for the rest of the game with Leith Parker returning to the touchline. Bush ran out 20–16 winners of this their last home fixture of the season.

TWICKENHAM LOSES ITS DECORUM

TWICKENHAM, FEBRUARY 1958

The Fourth Wallabies who toured Britain, Ireland and France in 1957–8 are remembered as a curious Jekyll and Hyde party. Off the field, they were pleasant, personable young men who made friends wherever they went. But their methods on the field were often questioned, accusations of over vigorous play being levelled against them from as early as the third match of the visit – an unexpected defeat at the hands of a young Cambridge University side.

The tourists were also dogged by injuries, the most serious of which was to Jim Phipps, their first-choice centre who broke his leg. It meant that the teenager, Jim Lenehan, who was originally selected as understudy to Terry Curley at full-back, had to be used as a first choice centre for the majority of the tour.

Lenehan was a prodigious left-footed kicker and a devastating tackler and it was one of his tackles in the match at Swansea that nearly sparked off a riot. He crashed into the little Swansea fly-half, Bryan Richards, with a late tackle in the second half that incensed the local crowd. There were catcalls and boos every time Lenehan received the ball after that, and many flare-ups among the players led to flying fists and misplaced boots. The wonder of it all was that nobody was sent off.

Lenehan was again the centre of controversy when the Wallabies played against England at Twickenham. The crowds at Headquarters have always had a reputation for enjoying their champagne parties in the car park before behaving sedately during even the roughest of matches. But for the first time Twickenham lost its decorum when the young Australian slid knees-first into England left wing, Peter Thompson, who had already been flattened by a tackle. This incident took place early on in the match at the south-east corner of the ground and it so roused the crowd that they, like the spectators at Swansea, subsequently booed Lenehan every time he became involved in the match.

This unprecedented behaviour by the crowd marred the match according to the press. The booing was 'of an ugliness even old campaigners could not recall previously at Twickenham,' reported Denys Rowbotham for the *Guardian*.

As the game developed, more and more of England's backs were in the wars. Jeff Butterfield was three times late tackled, Phil Horrocks-Taylor was off for an hour with a calf injury, Jim Hetherington was concussed and Dickie Jeeps bruised his right hand. Only Malcolm Phillips in the centre escaped lasting injury.

Fortunately at the end of the match there was one of those sporting moments when time stands still and every pulse quickens. In the dying minutes, the crocked England back division managed to ship the ball out to the right wing where Peter Jackson gathered on the Australian 25. Swerving past defenders and handing off would-be tacklers he beat a path for the corner where he leapt with a do-or-die dive for the winning try. The crowd erupted with joy, quickly forgetting the ugly scenes of the previous hour. In their jubilation they perhaps felt vindicated.

The match, always remembered for the Jackson try, nevertheless shocked the sporting fraternity. Even the well-known *Daily Express* cartoonist, Roy Ullyett, ended his strip with a record of the day that 'the Twickenham crowd went all common and booed'.

PLEASE CAN WE HAVE OUR BALL BACK?

COVENTRY, FEBRUARY 1958

The last match played by the Fourth Wallabies in England was against the Midland Counties at Highfield Road, the ground of Coventry City football club. The match play was not particularly distinguished, although the home side, comprising 13 Warwickshire players, did achieve its first win over a touring team for 30 years.

The bare playing surface, which in wet conditions churned into a mud-bath, did not ease the running and handling for the backs of either side, though both XVs did attempt to play open rugby. Coventry scrum-half George Cole put the Midlands ahead with a left-footed penalty goal after 20 minutes and Ron Harvey equalised early in the second half with a similar score for the Wallabies.

Fenwick Allison, an England full-back and the home side's captain, won the match ten minutes later when he was up in support of a three-quarter move and took an inside pass from wing Peter Jackson to score wide out. Cole converted to conclude the scoring: an 8–3 win for the Midlands.

If the play was forgettable, one moment stood out. A hugely entertaining episode of farce made this match a memorable one for the 10,000 who saw it. George Cole and Fenwick Allison on the home side together with Jim Lenehan and Terry Curley in the Australian XV were four of the most prodigious out-of-the-hand kickers of a rugby ball playing in the late 1950s. Twice during the early stages of the game match balls were kicked on to the top of the Highfield Road stands where they remained.

But when Allison had lodged a third ball on top of the roof, play ground to a complete standstill. Only three balls had been provided for the game and, this being a football ground, there were no spare or practice rugby balls lying around anywhere.

Allison himself, together with a couple of policemen, made earnest enquiries as the crowd became restless at the lack of action on the pitch. Eventually the long-suffering spectators were provided with the best entertainment of the afternoon. There was no alternative but for the groundstaff to march on to the pitch with an enormous ladder and clamber up to the roof. This brought light relief to the crowd, who burst into laughter and began clapping as a full-scale operation to recover the balls began.

While the intrepid groundsman spent five minutes recovering three rugby balls from the roof, a spectator tossed a souvenir miniature one on to the field, where it was enthusiastically received by the Australians who proceeded to further amuse the crowd with a mock game.

SEVEN SHIRT CHANGES

SWANSEA, APRIL 1958

For the greater part of the twentieth century the curtain came down on the representative season in Britain with the traditional Barbarians' Easter visit to South Wales. In its heyday the tour comprised four matches: Penarth on Good Friday, Cardiff on Easter Saturday, and Swansea and Newport on Easter Monday and Tuesday respectively.

The match at Swansea in April 1958 was described as the most ragged in Barbarians' history. Not because it was a scrappy game that did not come alive until the final ten minutes, but because of the numerous stoppages for shirt changes. All told, seven Barbarian shirts had to be replaced with Gordon Waddell, their young Scotland fly-half, having three jerseys ripped off his back.

The Scot shook off the rough-housing in the second half and brought a dreary match to the boil with a 30-yard (27.4-m) run through a forest of defenders to send Welsh lock Roddy Evans over for a try. Arthur Smith had kicked an earlier penalty.

The Barbarians were thus 6–0 ahead as the game moved into injury and jersey-changing time at the end. Swansea scored during the extra time when centre Gordon Lewis ripped through a gap to send flanker Ron Lloyd, a gentleman of the cloth who had been described as a fine example of muscular Christianity, in for a try that Dai Parkhouse converted. Final score: Swansea 5, Barbarians 6, Torn jerseys 7.

FRANCE CLAIM WORLD CROWN

JOHANNESBURG, AUGUST 1958

The path-finding French tour of South Africa in 1958 received little coverage in the British newspapers, yet it was one of the most significant events in the history of international rugby. For a start, it was the first short tour by a northern hemisphere union to the south. But the surprise outcome was that South Africa lost a home series for the first time since 1896, the victory by the French in the second Test announcing their arrival as a major force in world rugby.

The tour included ten matches, two of which were internationals, but the Test series caught South African rugby in confusion. The Springboks had ruled the roost of world rugby, home and away, from 1896 until sharing the series with the Lions in 1955. This was then followed by a disappointing tour of New Zealand in 1956 when the 'Boks' lost their first ever Test series to the All Blacks. When the French arrived, South African rugby was at a cross-roads, suffering in particular from a dearth of attacking half-backs. Even so, any thoughts of losing to the French were simply not entertained: South Africans did not lose Test rugby series on their own soil, especially against the French who were regarded on the veldt as the Cinderellas of world rugby.

As it turned out, the result of the series underlined South Africa's drop from its high estate. In the first Test in Cape

Town, South Africa's makeshift fly-half, Ian Kirkpatrick, adopted dour tactics. Time and again good possession went to waste through unimaginative kicking and the French were pleased to draw a match that they could even have won.

For the second Test, the South African selectors made seven changes and one positional adjustment. Although they led by a converted try to a penalty goal at half-time, the Springboks were outplayed in the set-pieces after the interval and a couple of dropped goals carried France to the most unexpected series win of the century.

News of the French success took precedence over all other sports news on Radio France and in the French press. 'Most sensational victory in the history of French rugby,' was the lead story in Paris's *Dimanche Soir*. 'France become world champions,' announced *Paris Presse* on its front page.

And to think, France had never even won the Five Nations outright before this tour. The South African adventure certainly stimulated interest in rugby throughout France and in the season that followed the French carried off the International Championship title for the first time. They were to remain European champions for four seasons.

GAME THAT STARTED A DEBATE

DUNEDIN, JULY 1959

Ever since Billy Bancroft landed the first one in an international in 1893, the penalty goal was referred to as the game's illegitimate child. By the 1950s more and more big matches were being decided by penalty goals, prompting a growing number of rugby's administrators and press critics, to campaign for a change to the laws of the game.

It was against this background that the Lions set off for New Zealand to meet the All Blacks in a four-match Test series in 1959. New Zealand had uncovered a prodigious place kicker in Don Clarke three years earlier. The Don had come into their side midway through an exciting series against the Springboks, and his place kicking had played a significant part in New Zealand's subsequent Test series win, their first ever against South Africa.

Clarke was the world's number one goal kicker when the 1959 series opened and the visiting Lions knew that he, more than any other New Zealander, was the biggest threat to their winning the series. They weren't wrong.

For the first Test, the Lions selected a back division that had all the talents. Ken Scotland was the best attacking full back in the four Home Unions, Peter Jackson and Tony O'Reilly on the wings would have been the automatic choices for any World XV of the day and Dickie Jeeps, the India-rubber man at scrum-half, was the most courageous half back in the game. They thrilled New Zealand crowds with their panoply of skills on that tour and were prominent in giving the Lions a 9–6 half-time lead in the Test played on the Carisbrook ground at Dunedin.

The Lions started the second half positively and in the next 25 minutes added tries by Peter Jackson and Welsh centre, Malcolm Price. In between, Don Clarke had kicked the All Blacks' third penalty goal so that, with a quarter of an hour to go, the Lions were 17–9 clear, having scored four tries to three penalty goals. New Zealand had never threatened their guests' line and seemed content to wait for the penalties to come Clarke's way.

The usually partisan New Zealand crowd were venting their displeasure at the manner in which the All Blacks were approaching the Test. Even their forwards, who admittedly were handicapped by injuries to two of their back row, found the Lions pack a handful. A penalty for a dubious offence offered Clarke the chance to reduce the deficit and with a siege gun kick the big full back sent the ball straight as a die between the uprights from 50 yards. A few minutes later and from a similar distance he brought the score back to 17–15 with a penalty after a line-out offence. Even the New Zealand crowd were cheering the Lions on now, cries of 'Red, Red, Red' regularly rising from the spectators packed into the tight Carisbrook enclosures.

Referee Allan Fleury, in his only international appointment, caught Gordon Wood (father of current Ireland hooker, Keith) offside at a ruck 30 yards (27.4m) from the posts five minutes from time. Clarke stepped forward to land another goal and thus clinched the match for New Zealand. At 18–17, the All Blacks had scored six penalties to four tries.

As the Lions attacked desperately for the winning score in the closing minutes, the onlookers got even more firmly behind them. The doyen of New Zealand press critics, Terry McLean, observed: 'The crowd in its shame called again for the Lions to win.' A last minute Lions attack carried play to the New Zealand line where a shrill blast on the referee's whistle led those supporting the tourists to think that a richly deserved fifth try had been awarded. But no. Instead, the referee had spotted another Lions offence, ruling that Roddy Evans had handled in a loose scrum, and with virtually the last act of the afternoon Clarke booted the ball into touch.

Then began the inquests. More than 20 penalties had been awarded during the course of the match: 14 to the All Blacks and seven to the Lions. 'We wuz robbed,' said the British critics following the tour. Welsh journalist Bryn Thomas, barely concealing his disappointment in a byline for a New Zealand newspaper, wrote, 'Today's match will certainly live on as one of the most exciting and, indeed, unusual of all time.'

Even parts of the New Zealand media sympathised. Referring to the penalties that resulted from technical offences, Fred Boshier in the *Evening Post* concluded, 'It is tossing too much into the lap of fortune when a purely involuntary action giving no advantage to a team carries a three-point penalty while a deliberately obstructive act pays the same price or even escapes scot-free.' Thus started the campaign that 17 years later led to the introduction of the differential (free kick) penalty.

As far afield as South Africa there was sympathy for the Lions. 'Lions lose – a crying injustice,' was the headline in one daily while Okey Geffin, who in 1949 had kicked five penalties for the Springboks in a winning Test against the All Blacks, spoke for thousands of like-minded neutral rugby followers when he said, 'A side which scores four tries and does not have its line crossed does not deserve to lose.'

The debate about the merits of changing the scoring values for penalty goals and tries was well and truly launched that day though it took another dozen years for the International Board to finally increase the value of the try to four points. Under that revised scoring system, the Lions would have taken this first Test 21–18 – which would have been a much fairer reflection of the run of play.

THE LONG ARM OF THE LAW TRIES TO INTERVENE

WANGANUI, AUGUST 1959

One of the hardest earned victories by the Lions in New Zealand in 1959 was against Wanganui. Bev Risman gave the tourists the lead with a penalty goal in the fifth minute but the determined hosts equalised when their wing, Boswell, landed a similar score. A tough, uncompromising forward battle developed in which no quarter was asked and certainly none was given.

Shortly before half-time Risman was given the opportunity to regain the lead for the Lions with a penalty awarded on the Wanganui 10-yard-line. As the English fly-half began making his preparations there was a commotion among the crowd on the far side of the pitch near the home side's 25. Unknown to the referee they were trying to draw his attention to the fact that the touch judge's flag was up to indicate that an earlier line-out had been awarded.

As Risman steadied himself to take the kick the baying from the crowd reached a crescendo. A policeman on patrol along the kicker's side of the field moved in at this stage and tapped the referee on the shoulder to point out the cause of the disturbance. The referee had lost sight of his touch judge in the far distance against the jumbled background of faces.

What followed was more extraordinary. The official permitted Risman to take his penalty and a low-trajectory kick just scraped over the crossbar. As the Lions withdrew to their half to receive the kick-off, the referee moved across to the touchline and spoke with the touch judge, whereupon he disallowed the penalty and whistled for a line-out.

The Lions and their small band of press followers were dumbfounded by these events and it was to the players' credit that they picked themselves up to grind out a narrow 9–6 win in the second half.

THE AMAZING MONSIEUR DROP

PARIS, APRIL 1960

Paris in the spring was a painful experience for many rugby international teams visiting either the old Stade Colombes or Parc des Princes for end-of-season Five Nations matches against the French. One of France's earliest April successes was against Ireland in 1960, when a side that was playing for a share of the International Championship title ran riot, winning 23–6.

The French played fluent rugby but it was the remarkable feat of hotelier Pierre Albaladejo that made the match a memorable one. The Dax fly-half, who after winning his first cap against England in 1954 had been in the Test wilderness until the Welsh match a few weeks earlier, sent over three sweetly struck drop goals, two with his left foot and one with his right. Never before in the annals of international rugby had a player planted three dropped goals in one match. One newspaper marvelling at his accuracy, described him potting 'with the mathematical certainty of a Joe Davis sinking the last three colours in an important break.'

Albaladejo later became the voice of French televised rugby until taking a well-earned retirement in 1999 after commentating on the Five Nations Championship's final weekend. But back in the spring of 1960, he must have created something akin to a record. For, apart from his well-publicised three goals in the Stade Colombes international against Ireland, he had a couple of weeks earlier landed four drops, two off each foot, playing for Dax in the Du Manoir tournament. Moreover, a week after his Paris exhibition, he popped over two more playing for France against Italy in Treviso.

Nine dropped goals in three matches: not bad for a player who was reported as having flat feet and fallen arches and who allegedly wore specially-supported shoes in everyday life.

ROLE REVERSAL

CARDIFF, FEBRUARY 1961

From the beginning the aim of the Barbarians, the world's best-known wandering rugby club, was to embrace imaginative and open rugby on the field with a spirit of comradeship and conviviality off it. This aim has remained the Barbarian ideal ever since.

In 1948 came one of the red-letter days in the club and rugby's history. The Third Wallabies of that year wished to return home via Canada, where they planned to put on a couple of exhibition games in British Columbia. To raise funds to assist the tourists' cause, the Four Home Unions committee met in Edinburgh and came up with the brilliant idea of inviting the Barbarians to select a team to meet the Wallabies. Club and international rugby in Wales immediately after the war had proved a compelling draw for returning servicemen, so the choice of venue for what was regarded as an experimental match was naturally Cardiff.

The game, played before 40,000 spectators, was a rip-roaring success and an exciting spectacle played according to the Barbarians' custom. It also set an important precedent: subsequent major visiting sides have always scheduled engagements with the club as their final tour match. The fixtures became cherished features of the Barbarian tradition and invariably turned out to be memorable exhibitions of attacking rugby – a shining example of the Barbarian ideal. With one notable exception.

The 1960–1 Fifth Springboks tour to Britain and Ireland approached their Barbarian match at the end of a long, unbeaten tour in which there had been criticisms levelled that an invincible record was more important to them than the manner in which they played the game. Playing power rugby together with the time-honoured South African principle of subdue and penetrate, the visitors had won few friends on tour despite compiling an enviable record.

During the winter of 1960–1 an influenza epidemic swept through Britain. The tourists did not escape and in the week before the final match of the British leg of their tour, injuries together with illness had decimated their squad.

So Ferdie Bergh, the Springboks' tour manager, suggested to the Barbarians that, instead of the normal challenge, the fit South Africans should integrate with a Barbarian selection and play a gala match on the Arms Park. Brigadier Glyn Hughes politely yet firmly replied for the Barbarians. 'The real attraction of this game is 15 South Africans against 15 Barbarians. In any case, as we have always stressed [in the Barbarians], the result is of minor importance,' he said.

Despite their difficulties with injuries and illness, the South Africans were still able to field a team with 12 Test players. Ironically, it was the Barbarians who suffered more through late withdrawals. The Welsh full-back Terry Davies dropped out with influenza, Cyril Davies withdrew through injury on the eve of the match, and two hours before kick-off the Irish scrum-half, Andy Mulligan, also went down with 'flu.

But such was the Barbarians' determination to win this match that they threw tradition to the wind. Under captain Ronnie Dawson, who had led the Lions in Australia and New Zealand two years earlier, they proceeded to play as if this were a fifth Test. Their tackling and defence work were watertight and it was significant that from an early stage in the match their halves, Richard Sharp and Billy Watkins, kicked as frequently as they would have done in a normal international. Gone was the ideal of attractive open rugby.

By contrast, and to their eternal credit, the Springboks ignored this defensive play and adopted the tactics more often associated with the Baa-Baas. They engaged in a wide passing game that won them many friends in a capacity 60,000 crowd. Ken Jones in the *Sunday Express* hit the nail on the head when he reported: 'We expected the dour Springbok approach to Test rugby and from the Barbarians the classical open football for which they are famous. But strange as it may seem the reverse happened. The Springboks opened up the game at every opportunity.'

Yet, despite living off emergency rations of possession, the Barbarians won a famous victory. Tries by Derek Morgan and Haydn Morgan in the eleventh and twenty-eighth minutes gave the club a 6–0 lead that was held until half-time.

As the Barbarians had shown so little in the way of adventurous running, the South African skipper Avril Malan continued to take the game to the club side in the second half. But twice Haydn Mainwaring, the uncapped Swansea replacement for Terry Davies, carried off try-saving tackles that went into the game's lore as two of the best of all time.

The first of these came when Malan, 15st (116kg)of prime South African beef, went galloping 30 yards (27.4m) down the south touchline from a line-out. Only the full-back stood between the Springbok captain and a certain try. Mainwaring lined his target up and bowled him into touch with a fair and perfectly timed shoulder charge that completely knocked the stuffing out of the big South African. Poor Malan lay prone in the Cardiff mud on the sidelines for the best part of two minutes before bravely continuing. Later, Mainwaring again saved the day for the Barbarians by bringing down Michel Antelme in open field. Consequently, the score remained at 6–0.

And so the Springboks lost their unbeaten record to the Barbarians but, as Vivian Jenkins summed up for *The Sunday Times*, 'They [South Africa] might well quibble that the Barbarians' alleged open football was something of a myth.'

MOTHER'S DAY

TIMARU, AUGUST 1961

Rugby can be an aggressive game at the best of times. With 30 young players all striving to establish themselves in the hurly-burly of a contact sport played at speed, is it any wonder that tempers are occasionally frayed? But when spectators get angry and become physically involved in the action on the field then the line has to be drawn.

During France's tour of New Zealand in 1961, the French team were embroiled in brawls in several games. Strong refereeing was often required to cool eager forwards as the temperature began to rise. One game in particular, against South Canterbury at Timaru, stood out for the rough play involved.

South Canterbury had never beaten a touring side but in front of 23,000 this was to be their day. Their mobile forwards completely disrupted the French, whose tour form hit rock bottom in this match and the home side, who ran out 17–14 winners despite finishing with only 14 men, led from an early stage.

Trouble broke out at the line-outs during the second half. Barging and pushing escalated into fisticuffs and it was the French who bore the brunt of referee Pat Murphy's ire. By the end of the game the penalty count went 17–4 against the tourists who were lucky not to have had a player sent off.

But the most astonishing incident occurred near the end of the match after South Canterbury's second five-eighth, Eddie Smith, was felled by a stiff arm tackle. Michel Crauste, the French captain, incensed the crowd further by picking the listless Smith up by the scruff of his neck and promptly dropping him back to the ground – whereupon a 56-year-old woman in the crowd rushed out from her seat, spoke to Crauste and clouted him on the back of his neck with her clenched fist. Two policemen had to intervene before escorting her, amid loud and approving cheers, from the field. Afterwards, the mother from Oamaru explained that she felt the tactics of the French team 'were totally uncalled for. I was so mad I did not know what I was doing. I hit him hard, but I don't think it hurt. I think he got a bit of a shock though.' Attending the match with her husband, two children and nephew, she added in her defence: 'It was not good for young boys to see that sort of play.'

Monsieur Crauste's reaction to the irate woman is not on record.

EIGHT TRIES FOR HEEPS

QUIRINDI, MAY 1962

To score eight tries in a match for your country is a phenomenal feat. It requires good hands, an eye for the opening and a good turn of speed. These were qualities which New Zealand's left wing, Rod Heeps, had in abundance when the All Blacks took on Northern New South Wales early in their tour to Australia in 1962. The visitors went on to register the first ton of points by a nation on a major tour, and Heeps himself set the world record for most tries in such a match.

The welter of scoring began in the first minute when burly full-back, Don Clarke, landed a penalty goal. The Waikato wonder kicker finished the match with 23 points on a day when all but two of the New Zealand team were on the score-sheet.

Heeps, a 24-year-old pharmacist who played his provincial rugby with Wellington, was the New Zealand 100 yards sprint champion at the time. Sprinters do not always make ideal rugby wingers, but Heeps showed that he had cultivated all the skills that go to make a first-class rugby three-quarter. Apart from pace, he had a good eye for the gap, a strong swerve and made tackles of textbook rectitude in defence.

He scored the first try of the match at Quirindi in the eighth minute and, with scores coming thick and fast, he went over again four more times before the interval, by which time the score was 45–0. When the last of his three second-half tries was converted the New Zealanders reached 100 points. Don McKay finished the scoring with a try to make the final score 103–0: 22 tries (valued at three points each at this time), 17 conversions and a penalty goal.

Heeps's record stands to this day for a tour match by a major International Board (IB) country visiting another IB country. However, the player faded from the scene almost as quickly as he had arrived. The meteor of 1962, he played all five Tests for New Zealand against Australia that year but, despite appearing in the trials for the following season, he never again represented his country.

ARCTIC MATCH

CARDIFF, JANUARY 1963

It was the match that went down in the annals of the game as England's last win in Cardiff for 28 years. Yet at the time it was that great old English conversation point, the weather, that dominated the headlines before and after the match.

As Britain shivered through its coldest winter for 16 years, the sports-starved public wondered anxiously whether the Cardiff match would go ahead. For five weeks the football league programme and club rugby schedule had been virtually obliterated by snow and frozen grounds. The poor San Isidro Rugby Club from Argentina, who were undertaking a short tour of southern England, had spent their first Saturday shopping for duffel coats in Oxford Street, as they tried to keep the Arctic winter out of their bones, and the hardest battle they encountered throughout their tour was keeping warm.

The Cardiff groundsman, Albert Francis, helped by staff from nearby Ninian Park and volunteers from the South Wales branch of the National Association of Groundsmen, ensured that the match would go ahead. They removed an overcoat of 30 tons of straw from the pitch on the morning of the match, leaving a thin layer to protect the turf against the biting wind until an hour or so before kick off. Workmen toiled hard to salt the terraces and clear snow so that the capacity crowd could be safely accommodated. The dead ball lines, however, were shortened to only 6 yards (5.5m) from the goal lines because of frozen patches near the east and west terraces. Indeed, during the pitch preparations the paint used for marking out the lines had frozen.

The players' preparations for the match did not go smoothly. The Welsh side were unable to find any surface in Cardiff on which it was safe to hold a training session, though down at Porthcawl the England squad donned pullovers, scarves and tracksuits for a runabout on the sands. England reaped the benefit of that workout the next day, their XV appearing better able to cope with the conditions than the rustier Welsh. On the afternoon of the match itself, the National anthems were played in the absence of the teams so that the players did not have to stand around in the cold, but could start the game immediately they marched out. The sides were issued with thermal underwear and the Welsh backs were offered mittens. The match attracted a huge television audience and turned out to be a fascinating affair. The temperature was measured at minus six at kick off and the pitch began to freeze early on, causing players to slip and slide but adding to the excitement for spectators. Wales had several chances to score tries in the first ten minutes but handling errors robbed them of points. England went ahead just before half-time with a try scored by Peter Jackson from a long Jim Roberts throw in and fully deserved their final 13–6 winning margin.

Afterwards the debate raged as to whether the match should have been played. Fortunately nobody was seriously injured, though several finished with cuts, grazes and friction burns. Only once since, when France and Ireland met in Paris in 1978, have ground conditions approached the concrete-hard danger of that Cardiff afternoon nearly 40 years ago. In Paris, it was the French Federation who overruled the concerns of players, Irish officials and the referee and insisted on staging the game. 'It was a miracle no one was seriously hurt,' said the Welsh referee on that occasion.

ONE HUNDRED AND ELEVEN LINE-OUTS

MURRAYFIELD, FEBRUARY 1963

The one ground in Britain where every rugby match was guaranteed to proceed during the Big Freeze of 1963 was Murrayfield. The Scottish Rugby Union in its wisdom had installed underground electric heating there a couple of years earlier ensuring that the playing surface for big matches was always excellent, no matter what weather conditions prevailed overhead.

Wales desperately wanted to win against Scotland in February 1963, having been beaten by England at Cardiff a month earlier while fielding an experimental XV that included six new caps. In particular, captain Clive Rowlands, who was one of those new caps, was determined to avoid leading Wales to two successive defeats.

As a leader he had a single-minded attitude to winning. Praise or scorn were irrelevant to him if his side was successful. He also wanted to dispel once and for all the theory that Murrayfield was a Welsh bogey ground. Four times since 1953, strong Welsh XVs had journeyed to Edinburgh expecting victory only to return narrowly defeated.

For bedtime reading on the eve of the match the Welsh captain chose to study the match programme for the game. Totting up the masses of the two packs he discovered that their published statistics measured up roughly even (121st 2lb (769kg) against Wales's 121st 9lb (772kg)). Getting out of bed, he roused his forwards to check their weights and discovered that the two Abertillery back-row men, Alun Pask and Haydn Morgan, had had their figures considerably understated. Wales, Rowlands reckoned, would take the field with a pack that was in the region of 2st (13kg) heavier than the Scots.

There and then he formulated his match plan: Wales would keep the ball among their forwards whose superior physical presence would almost certainly deliver the much-sought victory.

Rowlands, an extrovert personality whose energetic captaincy was always full of colourful gesticulations, totally ignored his backs in a match that yielded 111 line-outs – the record number for any international match. Time and again Rowlands hooked the ball into touch to push his side into Scottish territory. A Welsh supporter among their 10,000 travelling fans on Murrayfield's lofty banks was overheard saying, 'Rowlands has six signals for his backs: every one means he's going to hoof the ball back to touch.'

Wales took root in the Scottish 25 for most of the afternoon and won 6–0, Rowlands himself dropping a goal from a difficult angle in the second half. But the unattractive nature of the victory did prompt an outcry afterwards.

HANCOCK'S HALF MINUTE

TWICKENHAM, MARCH 1965

Who scored Twickenham's most famous international tries? Old timers still claim that the two scored by the Russian Prince Alex Obolensky against the 1936 All Blacks on England's way to a 13–0 win would take some beating. Peter Jackson's sensational last-minute try to seize victory against the Fourth Wallabies in 1958 is still talked of today, and then there was Richard Sharp's Championship winner when he sold three outrageous dummies in the 1963 Calcutta Cup encounter. Those with shorter memories might plump for the breathtaking French try started by Pierre Berbizier and Serge Blanco on their own dead-ball-line, and finished by Philippe Saint-André under the England goal in the 1991 Grand Slam showdown.

Yet arguably the most memorable out of the blue solo effort was the 95-yard (87-m) run by left wing, Andy Hancock, for England against Scotland in 1965. Scotland were leading 3–0 through a David Chisholm dropped goal and heading for their first Twickenham win since 1938 as play entered the final minute. None of the press photographers at the match rated England's chances of pulling the match out of the fire. All of them were camped in England's 25, expecting another Scotland score to seal the game.

Scotland's right wing, David Whyte, launched an attack and cutting in found himself engulfed by English forwards about 15 yards (13.7m) in front of England's posts. A maul developed enveloping Whyte and the ball was fed back on the England side to Mike Weston, their fly-half whose main function during the afternoon had been to hoof the ball into touch. Moving left to the blind-side, he threw a pass to Hancock who was standing in isolation near the left touch line.

It was only the third pass of the match that the Northampton wing had received: he'd dropped the other two. This time he latched on to the pass and began running up the left wing. He swerved outside the Scottish back row, evaded an ineffective tackle by the Scotland full-back and raced 90 yards (82.3m), hotly pursued by Iain Laughland, before lunging desperately over the line at the north end of the ground, just as the despairing Laughland completed his tackle. It was the longest solo run for a try ever seen in an international and saved England's bacon. 'I remember being helped up off the ground,' Hancock later recalled, 'but little else. On the way to the dressing room one of the spectators offered me a dram, which I gratefully accepted.' Unfortunately, with the cameramen stranded in Hancock's wake, no press photographs of one of rugby's most famous scores exist. The only record of the try is the grainy BBC film of the move.

REFEREEING HISTORY

PARIS, MARCH 1965

Frenchmen have figured prominently in the refereeing sphere of the game in recent times. Joel Dumé and Didier Mené have been regular appointments at International Championship matches in the past decade and, before them, Georges Domercq and Francis Palmade brought a Gallic touch to the Five Nations' tournaments of the 1970s and 1980s. Respect for fair play and imaginative use of the advantage law have been the common factors running through these well-known referees' approach to important matches.

Yet before 1966 no French referee had been invited to control an international game in the Home Unions tournament. It is true that Cyril Rutherford, the administrator who did so much for French rugby in the first half of the twentieth century, did appear as a touch judge in many of France's early internationals and actually controlled the France-England game in Paris in 1908, but he was actually Scottish born. And later, there was Jacques Muntz who was invited to referee the Four Nations match featuring England and Wales against Scotland and Ireland in 1929, when the Rowland Hill memorial gates were officially unveiled at Twickenham, but he never officiated in a Five Nations game.

In fact, it was only a fluke incident which led to French officials joining the rota for Championship games. During the 1965 France-Wales match at Stade Colombes in Paris, Ron Gilliland of Ireland had to relinquish the whistle just before half-time when he burst a blood vessel in his left calf muscle. Pure farce followed.

Welsh and French officials joined the captains on the field to decide what course of action to take. There was no precedent nor contingent provision: this was an unknown predicament for international rugby officials. As the protagonists engaged in a prolonged and energetic debate, the presidents of the French and Welsh Unions became involved in the pandemonium, as well as the chairman of the Welsh selectors, Alun Thomas. Meanwhile, an excited party of press photographers and television camera crews strayed on to the pitch to record developments.

Touch judges at international matches up to the mid-1980s were nominated by the two participating nations. Ron Lewis for Wales and Bernard Marie of France were on duty on this occasion and were duly brought into the discussions on the field. Both were highly respected referees, but either could be considered to be biased if they took charge of the match.

The Welsh skipper, Clive Rowlands, was particularly concerned that the choice of referee should be seen as fair and unbiased as Wales, already winners of the Triple Crown, were a staggering 13–0 behind in their quest for the Grand Slam. He felt that the direct choice of a Welsh referee might infuriate the French crowd and thus pressed the point that, for fairness, the captains should spin a coin.

At length, Alun Thomas provided the voice of reason. France, as hosts he argued, had nominated the match referee, therefore they should choose the replacement. Amidst catcalls and whistles, the French touch judge was nominated and, after a ten minute interruption, play eventually resumed.

And so Monsieur Marie, a chief of the legal department with the Bank of France, took over to become the first

Frenchman to officiate in the Five Nations Championship. His calm authority and scrupulous impartiality during the remainder of the match impressed everyone. 'The French referee did well,' acknowledged Clive Rowlands after his side had been beaten 22–13.

So well, in fact, that Monsieur Marie was rewarded with a full match in the Championship the following season when England met Ireland at Twickenham. Ever since, Frenchmen have been in demand at Test level, but one wonders how long it would have taken the authorities to extend this overdue invitation had Mr Gilliland not broken down in Paris on that March afternoon 35 years ago.

THE BATTLE OF WALDRON'S EAR

OXFORD, OCTOBER 1966

Ear-biting has brought damaging publicity to rugby at frequent intervals during the second half of the twentieth century.

Soon after the last war a brutal France-Wales clash in Paris was swept under the carpet at a time when investigative journalism had not spread to the sport. Legend has it that the Welsh prop who was the victim on that occasion formed a good friendship with the biter, and the players annually exchanged cards that read: 'Merry Christmas and a Happy New Ear.'

More recently, of course, the infamous Tetley's Bitter Cup tie between Bath and London Scottish in which the Exiles' flanker, Simon Fenn, was bitten on his left ear resulted in a protracted period of wrangling that did nothing for the reputation of the game. By then, of course, the game had turned professional and rugby union was forced to take action. It did, finding Bath prop Kevin Yates guilty and banning him for six months.

Even by 1965, when a Welsh forward allegedly bit an England player during a maul at Cardiff Arms Park, the authorities' attitudes had hardened considerably – to the extent that the Welsh Rugby Union took the then unprecedented step of dropping the alleged biter for the remainder of a Triple Crown campaign.

But, for immediate and drastic action taken after such

an incident, the battle of Waldron's Ear that took place at Oxford in October 1966 marked a watershed in the game's approach to dealing with foul play.

Ollie Waldron was an Ireland forward studying nuclear physics at Merton College when he was selected to prop for Oxford University against the 1966 Wallabies. It was only the third match of the visitors' tour and they had already lost once when they turned out at Iffley Road for a mid-week match.

The students, inspired by their South African captain Tom Bedford, began confidently and opened a nine-point lead in the first 12 minutes. Australia had to wait until the second half before scoring. Jim Lenehan, their captain for the day, made a well-timed entry into the three-quarter line and the upshot was a try for scrum-half John Hipwell which Lenehan, from a wide angle, converted. The Aussie captain made another incursion five minutes later to send Stewart Boyce over in the corner, and then put his side ahead after 15 minutes with a sweetly-struck dropped goal from half-way.

Thereafter, at 11–9, the match was as tight as the score suggests. Five minutes from the end came the incident that sent this game into the history books. From a scrum, Ollie Waldron emerged with a torn ear. He promptly left the field and was taken to hospital where he lost count of the number of stitches inserted in his ear-lobe.

It later emerged that Ross Cullen, the Wallaby hooker, had experienced such a torrid time in the front-row as a result of Waldron's illegal boring tactics that he had taken the law into his own hands. Waldron later stated that Cullen had threatened to bite him if he persisted in his tactics, whereupon he felt the Australian's teeth sink into his left ear-lobe.

After the match neither the referee, Peter Brook, nor Bill McLaughlin, the Wallabies' manager would comment on the incident. McLaughlin, who at the outset of the tour had promised to deal briskly with any foul play perpetrated by his team, was true to his word. The day after the match, in an unprecedented statement, he announced: 'I have decided that one of my players cannot be relied upon to carry out the firm decision of the Australian rugby touring management to play good clean rugby during the tour of the British Isles. I have therefore reluctantly decided that the player, Ross Cullen, will return at once to Australia.'

Mr McLaughlin's act was fully supported by his Union and acclaimed all-round by sports administrators and the media. 'It is easily the most significant decision ever taken in the interests of clean rugby and will have a salutary effect on the rest of the tour,' wrote the rugby correspondent of the *Daily Telegraph*.

On the evening of the announcement, as Cullen boarded the Alitalia flight for Sydney via Rome at London Airport, he vowed that he would never play rugby football again, adding, 'It's all very unfortunate but I must accept the decision.'

Back in Queensland, Cullen's home state, there was a feeling that their man was being made a scapegoat. He had never previously been involved in dirty play during a junior and senior career spanning 13 years and a week after his departure from Britain his Eastern Districts club in Brisbane unanimously reappointed him as their captain for 1967. But Cullen stuck to his word. He never played again and disappeared from the rugby scene.

THE UNBELIEVABLE DEBUT

CARDIFF, APRIL 1967

The Welsh rugby selectors have never flinched from throwing a good young 'un into the lion's den of Test rugby. The history of Welsh successes down the years is littered with the heroic feats of teenagers. Haydn Tanner against the All Blacks in 1935, Lewis Jones at Twickenham in 1950, Terry Davies against Scotland in 1953 and Terry Price in the Welsh Triple Crown year of 1965 were all barely out of Secondary School rugby when they confidently stamped their class on the international game.

But perhaps there was never a Five Nations debut that matched the performance of 18-year-old Keith Jarrett against England at Cardiff in 1967. The Newport player had left Monmouth School only a couple of months earlier before finding himself selected in the unaccustomed position of full-back for an international against an England side that was seeking the Triple Crown. A centre three-quarter by inclination and experience, Jarrett was chosen out of position by a Welsh selection committee that was desperate to accommodate a reliable place kicker.

Young Jarrett did not let them down. He was an old-fashioned, straight-on place kicker who tended to tilt the ball forward as he teed it up. He kicked his first penalty from near the left touchline early in the match. The ball appeared to be veering away to Jarrett's right before striking a post and bouncing over the crossbar. After that, the boy could do no wrong. The goal gave England a taste of what was to come.

Wales led 14–6 at half-time but by midway through the second half they were only four points ahead at 19–15, with England growing in confidence. Then England won a line-out in front of the south stand at the Westgate Street end of the ground and, from his own 25, Colin McFadyean, the English centre, kicked high towards his opponents' half with a kick designed to test the inexperienced Welsh full-back. Positionally, Jarrett was completely exposed. He had stood too far back to take the ball on the full and had no option but to let it bounce high on the half-way line. The English three-quarters and loose forwards were steaming across the field, hoping to take advantage, when Jarrett shot into view and perfectly timed his run to take the ball on the bounce and set off full pelt along the north touchline.

On and on he pounded with scarcely a hand laid on him. Once into the 25 it was obvious that no one would catch him and with no Welsh player in support he completed his 50-yard (45.7m) solo effort with a try in the corner that brought the house down. To add insult to injury, Jarrett converted from the touchline, bouncing the ball over off the top of an upright.

By the end of normal time Wales were 34–15 ahead, though England managed two late scores in injury time to add a touch of respectability to the result. Jarrett kicked seven goals from eight attempts – his one failure of the afternoon hit a post – and equalled the Welsh international record for most points (19) in a match, set by Jack Bancroft against a fledgling French side 57 years earlier.

The only comparable Test debut by such a youngster was made by the New Zealand wing Jeff Wilson against Scotland at Murrayfield in 1993. Brought on tour more for the experience than as a front line Test player, Wilson found himself promoted to the Test team at barely 20 years of age and scored a hat trick of tries in a record 51–15 walloping.

FOUR DRAWS IN FIVE MATCHES

HARTLEPOOL, APRIL 1967

The first county rugby match was staged at Leeds in 1870 with Lancashire defeating Yorkshire by a goal and two tries to nil. In 1883, regulations governing playing qualifications were agreed by the English counties and in 1889 the first championship officially sanctioned by the Rugby Football Union was introduced. Yorkshire were the inaugural winners.

The first formal structure to the Championship was imposed the following year: the north-east, north-west, south-east and south-west produced four group winners who then met in a league round to produce a title winner. In 1895 the structure was modified to produce a knockout phase which led to a final tie.

The competition produced its hundredth climax in June 2000, but the most unusual run of results in its colourful history came in 1967 when Surrey were the finalists with Durham. Draws have always been rare in senior rugby but that season the Surrey side featured in four draws in their final five matches. They had also drawn earlier in the season with Middlesex in the regional league.

Their semi-final was against Cornwall. The Duchy always treats its county side with the same respect that the rest of England reserves for the national team. (Indeed, nowadays the Twickenham authorities pray for Cornwall to reach the final every year to ensure a bumper gate.) Matters were no different in 1967 when Surrey journeyed west to Redruth on 4 February for their first showdown with Cornwall.

At the time Cornwall were spoilt for choice at full-back where they had at their disposal Roger Hosen and Graham Bate, two fine players with differing talents. Hosen was the England full-back at the time and a siege gun kicker who could place goals from anywhere inside his own half. Bate was more agile about the field but a less accomplished kicker. In the event, Bate was given the nod for the Redruth match.

The match went down in Cornish lore as the one that got away. The western county scored two tries but Bate's big failure with six kicks at goal – two conversions and four penalties – cost Cornwall dear. For big Bob Hiller, with a couple of penalty goals for Surrey, retrieved the draw and enabled the visitors to live to fight another day.

Hosen was recalled for the replay a fortnight later at Richmond. And it was a good job too, as far as Cornwall were concerned. Surrey took a 14–3 lead before Cornwall staged a magnificent comeback and, with the last act of the game, Hosen landed a touchline conversion to square the scores at 14-all. So it was back to Redruth for the second replay which, this time, Surrey comfortably won 14–3, to reach their first final for seven years.

Having reached the final, Surrey were involved in two further draws. The final against Durham took place at Twickenham, where Bob Hiller kicked 11 of their 14 points in a drawn game. The replay in late April was staged at Hartlepool and when this ended scoreless, the two counties were called on by the authorities to discuss the next step, there being no such thing as extra time or penalty shoot-outs to produce instant winners in those days. The sides debated the logistics of another replay but, with only a week to the end of the official season, they decided to share the title. It was, everyone agreed, the most spectacular ending to a county championship campaign.

REFEREE SENT OFF

PLYMOUTH, NOVEMBER 1967

According to the Rugby Law book, the referee has the power to order off a touch judge who in his opinion is guilty of misconduct. It doesn't happen very often, but when it does you can bet the event will make news.

In November 1967, the Royal Naval Engineering College and Camborne were involved in a friendly club match at Plymouth. George Riches, a well respected referee, a regular official on the county championship circuit and a former member of England's international panel, was running the line for Camborne when there was a touchline incident.

A couple of forwards became entangled in a punch up and the well-meaning Riches dashed in to intervene. By the time he arrived on the scene, the two fighters were going at it hammer and tongs and he knew that in order to make his presence felt, he would have to separate them forcibly. So he put his arm around the offending College forward and tried to pull him back. An incensed College supporter ran on and jumped on Riches's back before joining in the fracas. The match referee then arrived and, misinterpreting the situation, told his touch judge that he was dismissing him for fighting. There was some confusion about the dismissal but it was confirmed later. 'The referee did send him off,' said the Camborne secretary, Arthur Kemp, after the match. 'But from what I saw of the incident this was not necessary. George was only trying to keep the peace.'

THE DROP THAT NEVER WAS

DUBLIN, MARCH 1968

Mike Titcomb of Bristol was a referee noted for his empathy with players during a career that took in eight major international matches between 1966 and 1972. There was an occasion in Dublin in 1968, however, when even he would be the first to admit that he had no empathy with the Irish crowd. The occasion was the Ireland–Wales match that season when he erroneously awarded a dropped goal to each side. The first of these was in the twentieth minute of the first half when Ireland, leading 3–0, went further ahead through a drop goal from 35 yards by their fly-half, Mike Gibson. The ball was touched in flight by Welsh flanker John Taylor, which should have invalidated the score, but Mr Titcomb ruled that the kick was good. Naturally, the Irish crowd did not object. Wales then pulled back a penalty goal, making the scoreline 6–3 at the break, and then equalised early in the second half with international rugby's most famous dropped goal that never was.

Gareth Edwards drop-kicked high towards the Irish posts. Practically everyone in the ground saw the ball curl at least a foot outside the upright, but poor Mr Titcomb signalled the goal. Edwards, with a cheeky piece of gamesmanship, had raised his arm high as if indicating a fine goal and the referee was clearly taken in.

The Irish players, unaware that the goal had been given, assumed their positions for a 25 drop-out. They then realised to their dismay that the Welsh team had retreated to their own half, expecting a restart from half-way. Eventually it dawned on the crowd that the goal had been awarded and, as a result, a near riot resulted. Bottles and cans were hurled on to the pitch as a crescendo of hoots, whistles and boos emanated from the Lansdowne Road enclosures. Play was held up for several minutes as spectators broke through the touchline cordons to remonstrate with the referee.

When play eventually resumed the Irish, clearly roused by the injustice, raised their game to a fever pitch and the Welsh were swept aside in the tight and loose. At length, in the ninth minute of stoppage time, Ireland's wing forward Mick Doyle crashed over for the winning try. The conversion failed but that did not matter as the whistle for no-side went immediately afterwards, leaving Ireland deserved victors by 9–6.

'I thought the ball had gone over,' Mr Titcomb innocently explained after receiving a police escort from the pitch to the safety of the dressing room at the end of the match.

At least justice was finally seen to be done that day, which is more than can be said for another match involving Wales, in 1978. In the second Test of that year's tour down under, the Grand Slam champions went down 19–17 to a late dropped goal by Australia's fly-half, Paul McLean, that was hotly disputed by the Welsh players, who protested that the kick had flown 6in (15cm) wide of the posts. The Australian referee would have none of it and ruled that the kick was good.

A REPLACEMENT'S HAT-TRICK

SYDNEY, JUNE 1968

Replacements for injured players were occasionally made in New Zealand–Australia Test matches, long before the International Board officially sanctioned their use in 1968. Indeed, as far back as 1907, three replacements were made in the Sydney Cricket Ground Test between the two nations.

Replacements were still permitted between them when, in the 1947 series, an interesting qualifying restriction to their use was made. Now the replacements could only come on before half-time, presumably to discourage abuse of the law. Incidentally, in the programme for the first Test at Brisbane that year, New Zealand listed ten reserves from whom to make any necessary replacements. Even today when replacements seem to come and go with great regularity, teams nominate only seven for internationals.

The use of replacements in Australian Tests ended with the election of the Australians to the International Board in 1949. It was perhaps fitting then, given their long history of using replacements, that the first Australia–New Zealand Test under the International Board's ruling (also at the Sydney Cricket Ground, in 1968) is remembered for the remarkable performance of New Zealand's substitute loose forward, Ian Kirkpatrick, who in the twenty-fifth minute became his country's first replacement since that 1947 series.

Kirkpatrick came on when Brian Lochore, the New Zealand captain, withdrew with a hamstring injury. Within ten minutes he had scored the first try of the match. In the second half he crossed for the last two tries of the afternoon, to become the first substitute to score a hat trick in a Test.

Kirkpatrick went on to become the most prolific try scoring forward in the history of Test rugby, though at the time of writing his record appears likely to be overtaken by England's Neil Back. Even so, in the intervening years the only other replacements to finish with three tries in a Test are Byron Hayward of Wales, who performed the feat against Zimbabwe on his debut in 1998, and Tiaan Strauss for Australia against Ireland in 1999.

One of the most unusual replacement tries in an international was scored by Maesteg's Chico Hopkins for Wales against England at Twickenham in 1970. Wales were trailing 6–13 when their star player, Gareth Edwards, was forced off through injury and on came little Chico for his only Welsh cap. First he created a blind-side opening for J.P.R. Williams to crash over and then he popped over himself for a try that was converted to put Wales ahead. But the unique point about Hopkins's score was that it was a replacement's try awarded by a replacement referee. Monsieur Robert Calmet, the French referee, had had to retire at half-time with a broken leg and England's Johnny Johnson had come on to deputise.

More recently, since the advent of blood bin substitutions, two performances warrant mention. Eddie Halvey created a piece of rugby history for himself in the 1995 Rugby World Cup when he came on as a temporary replacement for Denis McBride in Ireland's crucial pool match against Wales. While Halvey made his cameo appearance he scored a try that helped his side to a 24–23 win and qualification for the quarter finals. Even Halvey's feat, however, was surpassed a couple of years later when Australian Mitch Hardy managed two tries whilst deputising briefly as a temporary replacement for Stephen Larkham against France at the Sydney Football Stadium.

INJURED RUNNING OUT

PARIS, JANUARY 1969

Replacements were nominated for the Five Nations Championship for the first time in 1969. In the opening match of the campaign that year, France were mightily relieved to have a bench of ready-changed substitutes on hand when a stand-in for Jean-Pierre Salut, a blond flanker of Russian extraction, was needed slightly earlier than anticipated.

Salut was a sublime loose forward who had set the Five Nations alight with his dashing play in 1968 when France won their first Grand Slam. On tour with the Tricolores in New Zealand and Australia during the summer of that year he had fallen out with the management over what was referred to as 'his excessive individualism off the field' and, as a result, the French had dropped him for their three autumn internationals against the Springboks and Romania. But he was recalled for the championship opener with Scotland and his return was looked forward to with relish by the French rugby public as well as the critics.

Alas, he was to become the victim of one of international rugby's most unfortunate incidents. He twisted an ankle before leaving the dressing room and was apparently given a pain-killing injection. Then, as he was running out he was observed to go over on the ankle on the steps leading up from the tunnel to the field and fell heavily to the ground.

Later the story emerged that Salut had only gone on to the

field to show his face, for the theory held in some quarters of French rugby was that he was often a bit too quick to withdraw from international sides. It was clear, however, that he would be unable to take his place in this particular side, so the French were forced to call on one of their bench replacements even before the match started.

So, up from the bench stepped prop forward Jean Iraçabal and without batting an eyelid the French selectors proceeded to completely rearrange their scrum. Iraçabal was a specialist loose-head prop, so original selection Jean-Michel Esponda was shuffled across to tight-head. Michel Lasserre was moved from tight-head to second-row replacing Benoït Dauga, Dauga slipped back to the number eight slot where Walter Spanghero had been originally chosen, and Spanghero went across to fill the open-side position vacated by Salut. Five pack changes between leaving the dressing room and lining up for the National Anthem must surely be a record in a Test match. As Clem Thomas noted in *The Observer*: 'Only the French would make a change of such complexity.'

Scotland, however, showed their guts and won a match in which France displayed all their talent. A late try by Jim Telfer brought them a 6–3 win that was to be their last in Paris for 26 years.

THE GAME WITH A PUNCH

CARDIFF, MARCH 1969

Many Wales and Ireland matches down the years have been remembered more for their tough and uncompromising forward exchanges than the quality of the rugby. The 1914 showdown in Belfast, for instance, was often referred to as the 'roughest ever' by old timers. It was a game that featured a running feud between several members of the Irish and Welsh packs in which punches were exchanged off the ball and out of sight of the referee. The sides enjoyed their 80-minute scrap and though the result of the match soon became forgotten, the Welsh pack of that year who were led by the Rev. Alban Davies were for ever and a day referred to as 'The Terrible Eight'.

The modern equivalent to that ancient ritual was a less cavalier affair. In 1969, Wales entertained Ireland at Cardiff when the visitors were seeking the Grand Slam and Triple Crown for the first time for more than 20 years. Wales, with a new, young side that had beaten Scotland, were pioneering a squad system that season. It involved a group of 28 leading players who met regularly on Sundays under the beady eye of coach Clive Rowlands, who put the boys through their paces. The system courted controversy in the Home Unions, with the Irish being particularly outspoken about the professional approach adopted by the Welsh. Accepted practice at the time was for international teams to meet no more than 48 hours before kick-off times.

The Irish were not altogether lily white themselves going into the Grand Slam match. There had been allegations that the French and Scots had been battered into submission by the Irish forwards earlier in the season and when the sides lined up to meet Prince Charles, a guest of the Welsh Rugby Union in his year of investiture as Prince of Wales, few expected that the ensuing game would be a vicar's tea party.

The match erupted in the third minute when the Welsh captain, Brian Price, flattened Ireland's pack leader, Noel Murphy, with a right upper-cut that would have done Henry Cooper proud. The punch was thrown in front of the main grandstand and was clearly seen by millions watching the match on television. Surely the referee, Doug McMahon of Scotland, had no alternative but to issue the Welsh captain with his marching orders?

But Mr McMahon, who had been unwell during the morning with a stomach upset and very nearly cried off from refereeing the match, did not send the Welshman off. Price was a skilful lock who had a reputation for restraint. The referee sensed that he had been sorely provoked and instead issued a severe reprimand to the effect that the captain would be off if there was a repeat of his outburst.

Even Price's best friends thought he was lucky to stay on. Former distinguished Welsh referee, Gwynne Walters, was convinced afterwards that he should have been dismissed without further warning, though Price's subsequent statements went some way towards explaining if not justifying his actions. 'A player came over the top in a maul and his fingers were in my eyes. You don't hang about,' he said. Murphy denied that he had clawed Price.

The niggling persisted throughout the first half. Three Irish forwards, Murphy (again), Ken Kennedy and Jim Davidson needed further attention as the battle raged on and each finished the match suffering from concussion. Kennedy was indefensibly punched whilst pinned between his props in the front row of a scrummage. At one stage Ireland's captain, Tom Kiernan, threatened to march his side off. On the Welsh side, their big second row Brian Thomas was on the receiving end of a stray boot at the bottom of a ruck, and had to withdraw to have ten stitches inserted in a head wound, as undercover punching and gouging continued among the packs.

The better organised Welsh XV ran away to a 24–11 victory in the second half after trailing for much of the first. Yet the roughest match ever of the television age left a bitter taste as the arguments about foul play continued long after the result had been forgotten.

BUILDING SITE RUGBY

CARDIFF, APRIL 1969

No one could accuse the Welsh Rugby Union (WRU) of sitting on its laurels as far as developing the site at Cardiff Arms Park is concerned. At regular intervals since the 1930s the Union has invested huge amounts of money into capital redevelopments that have greatly benefited the rugby-loving Welsh public. The culmination, of course, is the spanking new Millennium Stadium that was unveiled for the 1999 Rugby World Cup. But the opening of the double-decker north stand (1934), the south stand upper deck extension (1956) and the ambitious rebuild that turned the Arms Park into a National Stadium worthy of that title in the 1970s were equally magnificent projects in their day.

The arrangements for the rebuild in the 1970s led to international rugby taking place against surely its oddest back-drop. The old north stand was pulled down over the summer of 1968 to clear the way for the first stage of the redevelopment – the construction of a new cantilever north stand. For the internationals of 1969, however, it meant that the ground had a reduced capacity of 29,000 on the remaining three sides of the pitch.

Wales's Triple Crown match against England in April that year took place on a ground that resembled a building site. Barbed wire fences had to be erected on the north side to keep out an expected crowd of gatecrashers and Cardiff Police joined Welsh Rugby Union officials and security experts to ensure that the perimeter fencing was not breached. The police also warned that trespassers would be ejected. Meanwhile, the contractors, Andrew Scott Limited, confirmed that their workmen would be engaged in the building of the new super-structure while the match was taking place – a situation that surely would not arise today when public safety is paramount. Press photographs of the game showed, unsurprisingly, that the workforce were more distracted by the events on the field than the job in hand.

So why didn't the Welsh Rugby Union make arrangements to shift the match to Twickenham instead? In 1998 and 1999, during the construction of the Millennium Stadium, they successfully decamped to Wembley Stadium, culminating in a famous win over England, robbing Martin Johnson's men of the Grand Slam in the last ever Five Nations Championship match.

But back in 1969, Welsh rugby was riding on the crest of a wave. Cliff Jones, chairman of the Welsh selectors, explained the decision to play on the Arms Park rather than in England thus: 'We studied this problem when we were making our arrangements for this season,' he said. 'We realised that it could turn out to be a very important game in this season's championship, but we considered it would be unfair both for our team and our supporters to turn a home game into an away one.'

And so Wales delighted their fans, winning their building site Test 30–9 to carry off the Triple Crown and Five Nations Championship.

THE SECRET AFFAIR

NEW BRIGHTON, NOVEMBER 1969

The Sixth Springboks to come to Britain and Ireland were the last official South African international team to visit these shores for more than 20 years. Their matches were played in difficult circumstances as protesters staged anti-apartheid demonstrations inside as well as outside the venues where they were scheduled to appear.

Even before the opening match of the tour, against Oxford University, the tourists had a taste of what was to come. Anticipating demonstrators, Oxford police informed the University Rugby Club that it would be unable to guarantee safe arrangements for a match at Iffley Road. It was touch and go whether the match would proceed, but on the eve of the fixture it was announced that Twickenham would stage the game.

Two groups of protesters arrived at the ground on the afternoon of the match. There was a peaceful demonstration outside the ground but a more militant group infiltrated the spectators inside to disrupt the match by blowing whistles. The game was surrounded by confusion, though a strong police cordon successfully restricted demonstrators from breaking onto the field of play.

Similar scenes followed the tourists more or less throughout the tour. At Swansea there were unpleasant violent scenes before, during and after the Springboks' game against the local club. By the time the South Africans were due to make their first visit of the tour to Ireland in late November, concerns were being expressed that the prevailing political troubles there, coupled with the threat of anti-apartheid disruption, would make the Ravenhill Ground in Belfast, where the tourists were due to play, the focus for violent groups. And so the scheduled tour match against Ulster was cancelled.

The Saturday that had been set aside for that game, however, was also the date when New Brighton, one of Northern England's most homely clubs, were due to entertain the North of Ireland Football Club, one of Ulster's oldest and most distinguished clubs. The tour committee secretly arranged for the clubs to forego their annual fixture and to field a combined XV that would face the Springboks instead. None of the players knew about the plans until the morning of the match. The game was played before a small crowd and went off without a hitch. It remains the only major tour match in the sport's history to be played in such secrecy.

The Springboks won 22–6 and their skipper, Dawie de Villiers, said afterwards that they had thoroughly enjoyed 'playing in a purely rugby atmosphere'. For once the tour demonstrators were absent, only learning that the game had been staged when they read the newspapers the next day.

The Springboks were to feature in an even more clandestine affair nearly a dozen years later in North America. On that occasion they were making a three-match visit to the United States after a full-scale tour of New Zealand.

In an effort to escape anti-tour groups, their international with the Eagles was hastily arranged for a secluded polo field in the country districts of New York. The pitch was littered with horse manure, the makeshift posts were rapidly erected before the match and just as quickly dismantled after it – preparations that were similar to those of a Sunday morning park match. It was recorded that 35 spectators, 20 policemen, a television crew, one pressman and no protesters attended.

KICK HIS CHAUFFEUR WHILE YOU'RE AT IT

TWICKENHAM, FEBRUARY 1970

Tony O'Reilly began his senior rugby career on the Dublin club rugby circuit in 1954. Within months his powerful running and resourceful defence for Ireland were the talk of the Five Nations. O'Reilly was Ireland's centre, but the 1955 Lions in South Africa used him primarily as a wing. That tour made him. The red-headed teenager who used his pace to turn defences inside out finished with 16 tries to his name and played a significant part in the Lions' 23–22 win in the Johannesburg Test.

More than 95,000 were present to see him stamp his name on that game. He created a try for Scotland's Jim Greenwood and ran like an express train to score another. The Lions subsequently shared the series before returning to a heroes' welcome. In addition to his play, O'Reilly's wit also made him a popular member of the tour party. Furthermore, his good looks turned the heads of adoring South African women on that tour. An 'I-touched-Tony' following developed and there was talk later of his being approached for a part in the remake of the movie Ben Hur.

O'Reilly also toured with the Lions in 1959 to Australia and New Zealand. Once again, O'Reilly the rugby player was the star attraction on the field and his 22 tries on that tour remains a Lions record. And once more, he was the star off the pitch as well. By now a junior solicitor, he featured prominently in representations to management over injustices felt by the players and his witty intellect continued to amuse his colleagues.

This magnetic personality and intellectual energy took him to great success in his business career and by the age of 30 he was manager of the Irish Dairy Marketing Board and he later became president of H.J. Heinz. His business interests in Ireland eventually made him that country's richest man and biggest employer.

However, as far as his rugby career was concerned, the widely-held tenet was that the best of his rugby was never seen in these islands. His Ireland career was interrupted by injuries and business commitments and by 1964 his international rugby days appeared to be over. Until, that is, he was dramatically called up on the eve of the 1970 Twickenham international against England when Ireland's original wing choice, Bill Brown, withdrew from the squad with an ankle injury.

At 33, O'Reilly was enjoying his social rugby with London Irish and had clearly lost the pace and stamina of an international class three-quarter. He was now considerably broader than on his Test debut 15 years earlier and after Ireland's eve-of-the-match run-out one of the squad confided that their warm-up run had involved 'running twice round O'Reilly'. The great man had actually written the lead article for the official match programme and had been invited by his old Lions colleague, Cliff Morgan, to help with the live BBC television commentary. On hearing of his sudden international recall O'Reilly announced that he was delighted to be back. His presence added another 5,000 to the Twickenham gate. It was hard luck, though, on the young travelling reserve Frank O'Driscoll of University College Dublin who, after getting so close, never won his cap for Ireland.

Unfortunately, O'Reilly spent most of the match in a daze having received a kick on the head after diving at the feet of England's pack. 'And while you're at it, why don't ya kick his chauffeur too,' remarked an Irish voice in the crowd. For O'Reilly, by then the European managing director of H.J. Heinz, had famously turned up for the pre-match runabout at the Honourable Artillery Club in central London in a chauffeur-driven limousine.

Despite his unremarkable play in that game, that extraordinary recall added another remarkable statistic to his file: an international career spanning 16 seasons, the world record for rugby union.

THE GREATEST CONVERSION SINCE ST PAUL'S

MURRAYFIELD, FEBRUARY 1971

The most pulsating match in Five Nations history was the Scotland-Wales clash at Murrayfield in 1971. A confident Welsh side that had annihilated England a fortnight earlier travelled north with nearly 20,000 of their fanatical supporters to meet a Scotland side that had fallen to a 13–8 defeat against France in Paris on the opening Saturday of the season.

The match took place in perfect conditions and the lead changed hands five times – three times in eight minutes during one stage of the second half – before, with Scotland ahead 18–14 with only a couple of minutes to go, Barry John opened the doors of the last-chance saloon by scrambling the ball into touch on the old grandstand side of the ground inside the Scottish 25.

With all Wales willing Delme Thomas, their lock, to lift his tired body for one last leap of the afternoon, the Llanelli linesman did his stuff admirably to intercept the Scottish throw and palmed the ball down to Gareth Edwards.

Out the ball went from Edwards and across the Welsh back division to Gerald Davies, who arced outside the defence for a wonderful try. The Scots did, however, manage to keep him hemmed in to the corner of the field, so that at 17–18 behind, Wales still needed the difficult conversion points to regain the lead. John Taylor, the London Welsh flanker, was entrusted with the all-important conversion and to maximise the angle took the ball out fully 35 yards (32m) before lining up his sights.

As the crowd on the old Murrayfield terraces waited in silence, Taylor took his measured run up and slammed the ball with his left foot. It sailed high and true between the posts: the most famous conversion since St Paul's on the Damascus road nearly 1,900 years earlier.

Gordon Ross, a well known freelance, waxed lyrical. 'Never, in the history of rugby football, will any man, woman or child who was caught in the emotions of this magnificent and nail-bitingly exciting game, ever forget it,' he reported in the *Playfair Rugby Football Annual*'s review of the season.

DOCTOR DOUG SMITH'S CRYSTAL BALL

AUCKLAND, AUGUST 1971

The Lions of 1971 trod new ground. Never before (nor since) had a British/Irish combination returned victorious from a Test tour of New Zealand. But, with a back division of unsurpassed brilliance, in which every player was a master of the game's basic skills, and a forward unit that was both physically and tactically a match for the All Blacks, the Lions managed to pull off a famous triumph.

The credit for the side's technical expertise went to Carwyn James, the Lions' coach from Llanelli. James allowed a wealth of different talents to mature into a team that admitted the free expression of genius within the carefully prepared match plans drawn up for each new challenge. James simply created a side that was dedicated to winning and was devoted to its coach.

Then there was Dr Doug Smith who led the tour's senior management. A Lion himself in 1950, he was the charismatic manager who guided the brilliant class of '71. In all walks of life, one of the hallmarks of successful managers is the ability to make the task challenging for their charges while easing the routine chores behind the scenes. Dr Smith was the perfect leader in this respect, effectively and efficiently smoothing the path the players trod on tour.

But what really amazed the Lions and All Blacks alike was Smith's crystal-ball gazing. He confidently predicted at the outset of the visit that the Lions would return winners of the series, forecasting a 2–1 margin with one Test drawn. Bearing in mind that no Lions side had ever succeeded in New Zealand and that in international rugby draws occur perhaps once in every 20 matches or so, this was a highly unlikely outcome.

Well, the Lions did win two Tests and were therefore already sure of a share of the series when they travelled to Auckland 2–1 up for the fourth and final Test in mid-August. That final Test went to the wire. It was 8–8 at the interval before Barry John nosed the Lions ahead with a penalty three minutes into the second half. Next, Bryan Williams made a searing break which led to an equalising New Zealand try scored by Tom Lister before J.P.R. Williams, with an extraordinary dropped goal from 45 yards (41m), restored the Lions' lead. Eight minutes from time, Laurie Mains kicked a penalty and, at 14–14, the match finished all square and the most extraordinary prediction in rugby history had come true.

ENGLISH RUGBY'S FIRST CUP FINAL

TWICKENHAM, APRIL 1972

For more than a century after its foundation in 1871, the Rugby Football Union (RFU) steadfastly rejected all manner of proposals for making the game in England more competitive. National leagues or knockout cups, it was argued, were not in the best interests of the game.

The year after the Union celebrated its centenary a pilot scheme was adopted to launch an RFU Cup competition for senior clubs. Squabbles regarding venues, kick-off times and even dates for arranging matches took some of the gloss off the inaugural event. But the Cup ties did bring together top sides who had never previously met and gave the club season a distinct climax. By the time that Gloucester and Moseley reached Twickenham for that first final in April 1972, the idea was embraced as a resounding success.

A crowd of 15,000 – not quite the 70,000 of the 1990s – turned up to witness the novelty of a Cup Final for the senior English rugby clubs. Gloucester, after coming through the more difficult half of the draw in which they defeated Bath, Bristol, London Welsh and Coventry, were deserving winners of that first final, beating Moseley 17–6.

The sole blot on the day was that Ron Lewis, the only Welsh referee who has controlled an RFU Cup final, had to dismiss Moseley's England lock, Nigel Horton, for punching. It was the first time for nearly 50 years that a player had been ordered off on a big Twickenham occasion.

ACTRESSES AGAINST MODELS

SUNBURY-ON-THAMES, SEPTEMBER 1974

The women's game is now very much a part of modern rugby. There is a thriving club scene in England and Wales, an annual Five Nations Championship and even a well-organised, four-yearly World Cup.

But things weren't always so structured in the women's game nor was it even accepted and taken seriously. As recently as 1974 the only women's matches likely to take place were charity games. One such game, staged at the ground of London Irish, featured a team of models against a team of actresses.

The coverage of the match deplored the lack of rough stuff and with sexist overtones reported: 'There was always the mirror. They stood in front of it at half-time repairing the damage to their carefully-prepared make-up.'

To add to the novelty of the occasion the girls played with two rugby footballs in the second half. 'It gave the fans two beautiful contests for the price of one,' it was recorded. Final score: Actresses 10; Models 10.

UP YOUR JUMPER

SYDNEY, MAY 1975

The late Daryl Haberecht was one of Australia's most gifted and innovative coaches. Apart from studying the Union game in great depth he was a keen observer of both League and American grid-iron tactics, and was not averse to pinching ideas from other codes that could be usefully tried in the Union game.

He achieved notoriety in May 1975 when, as the coach of the New South Wales Country XV, one of his well-rehearsed tricks led to a sensational last-minute win over arch-rivals Sydney. The score was 20–16 to the city slickers with time running out when the Country XV were awarded a penalty 44 yards (40m) from the Sydney goal-line.

John Hipwell, the Country XV's skipper, a veteran Test scrum-half and also Australia's captain at the time, was preparing to take a tap penalty when the Sydney side were confused by about a dozen of their opponents lining up shoulder to shoulder in a shallow crescent and with their backs to them. Hipwell was at the focus of the crescent and took the tap whereupon the ball was handed pass-the-parcel fashion along the line of players. The attackers further bewildered the Sydney players by making dummy movements as if handling the ball.

At Hipwell's signal every member of his team appeared to tuck arms under his jumper, turn and run in different directions towards the Sydney line. One of the players,

Greg Cornelsen, actually did stuff the ball under his shirt but after running for 11–16 yards (10–15m) realised that he would have to hold it properly.

Even so, the trick had its desired effect, causing mass confusion in the Sydney ranks as defenders wondered who had possession of the ball. They eventually picked up Cornelsen, the big country number eight, galloping towards them. Though challenged, the forward managed to make 33 yards (30m) before passing to Geoff Shaw who sent lock Brian Mansfield over near the posts. Referee Bob Fordham allowed the try and Country's fly-half, Jim Hindmarsh, landed the easy conversion to win the match 22–20.

Several sides tried to mimic the move in the weeks that followed before Australian referees referred the matter to the International Board, who ruled that the up-your-jumper tactic was against the spirit of the game and was therefore illegal.

Haberecht himself went from strength to strength. Within a couple of weeks of his side's infamous trick he masterminded their 14–13 win over Tony Neary's England touring team, and three years later he became Australia's coach. Taking the Wallabies to New Zealand in 1978, he unveiled a number of new tricks on tour, one of which was a variation on the up-your-jumper ruse. In the Test at Christchurch, John Hipwell arranged his team in a crescent at a tap penalty and feinted to pass. Simultaneously, his 14 colleagues began sprinting in different directions to confuse the All Blacks. Among the coach's other tricks was the 12–man scrum, while a more dangerous move involved the fly-half running up and over the backs of the forwards at a scrum. Sadly, Haberecht's national appointment was cut short owing to his ill-health.

THE REFEREE WHO FORGOT THE LAWS

MURRAYFIELD, JANUARY 1976

A refereeing error that may have changed the course of the match occurred at Murrayfield in January 1976 when Scotland played France on the opening Saturday of the season's Five Nations championship. The game was played on a windswept ground where place-kicking became a lottery.

Scotland opened the scoring when Dougie Morgan, their scrum-half, dropped a neat goal. After that the match became a battle of the kickers as both sides tried to score through penalty goals. Andy Irvine missed with a long-range effort before sending his next ball high over the posts to give Scotland what everyone believed would be a 6–0 lead. The Scots were sitting on a ten-match unbeaten record at Murrayfield and the crowd felt at this stage that the eleventh win of the sequence was in the bag. But to their dismay they realised that the English referee, Ken Pattinson, had disallowed the goal.

Because of the strong wind, Irvine had requested the help of a ball holder. Prop Ian McLauchlan offered his assistance and placed the ball for the successful kick, but in order to accommodate his kicker's round-the-corner style he had to lie in front of the ball to hold it. The referee ruled that McLauchlan was, therefore, offside at the time of the kick and ordered a scrum. It was a mistake. The laws of the game at this time clearly stated that in such circumstances the placer could be in front of the kicker.

Scotland eventually went down 13–6 to the French, but arguments raged over a decision that Mr Pattinson was man enough to admit was an error. Scotland felt that the 6–0 lead that the award of the penalty would have given them would have helped to lift their game. Poor Mr Pattinson never again took control of a major international match.

THE PRINTER'S NIGHTMARE

PARIS, MARCH 1980

Colm Tucker was a typical all-action Munster flanker who had the misfortune to arrive on the Irish Test scene while Fergus Slattery was an automatic choice on their back-row. Tucker's dynamic play was first noted by the wider rugby audience of the Home Unions when, in 1978, he was a member of the famous Munster XV that defeated New Zealand 12–0. He battled with an insuperable will to win and his determination eventually carried him into the Irish side for a couple of Five Nations appearances in 1979. A year later he became the first Shannon player to win selection for the Lions.

Early on he had to accept that some of the less enlightened copy takers on British newspapers would report his name inaccurately. No doubt he became used to seeing his name appear as 'Colin' in the English press reports.

Even he, though, must have raised an eyebrow when he opened the programme for the 1980 France-Ireland match in Paris. Nominated as one of the Ireland pack replacements for the match, he saw that his surname had been unwittingly misprinted by the French programme editors. The letter T was replaced with the letter F ... and so a proof-reader's nightmare became a programme collector's treasured item.

Mid-way through the first half he came on to replace John O'Driscoll. The French announcer heralded the substitute by referring to the programme and using 'that word', very much to the amusement of the Irish contingent in the crowd.

A TRY AWARDED IN ERROR

TWICKENHAM, MARCH 1981

France came to Twickenham in search of their third Grand Slam on the last Saturday of the 1981 Five Nations Championship. They were rather lucky to secure the title, a refereeing error enabling them to score a converted try that contributed to their winning margin.

There was a gale-force wind blowing when France won the toss and elected to make first use of it. Their fly-half, Guy Laporte, was the first to score with a long range dropped goal. Soon afterwards came the illegal move.

A quick throw-in on the England 22 resulted in Jean-Pierre Rives creating the space for his fellow flanker Pierre Lacans to canter over to the left of the posts for a try that Laporte converted into a 9–0 French lead. The try was awarded in error because the ball which Pierre Berbizier had used for the throw was supplied by a bystander. This contravened the relevant law, which stated that for a quick throw in the ball that went into touch must be used, that it must be handled only by the players and that it must be thrown in correctly.

The match, otherwise controlled with characteristic quiet authority by Allan Hosie, the respected Scottish referee, finished in a 16–12 win for France.

FLOUR BOMBS INTERRUPT PLAY

AUCKLAND, SEPTEMBER 1981

It was the oddest tour ever undertaken by the Springboks. Anti-apartheid demonstrations during their visit to New Zealand meant that the tourists were kept under strict security for the best part of six weeks. At times the Springboks were unable to leave their hotel rooms and there were occasions when late changes of plan necessitated their sleeping on sports-hall floors. At every match venue they had to run the gauntlet of protesters to fulfil their fixtures.

Two of the games were cancelled. At Hamilton, in the first week of the tour, more than 200 demonstrators ripped down a chain fence to break on to the pitch where they sprinkled tacks and staged a sit-in on half-way. The sides had changed and tossed for ends and a crowd of 25,000 was in place to see the Springboks take on Waikato. But the protesters defied the attempts of the police to disperse them and after an hour it was reluctantly decided by the organisers that the match should be cancelled. Thereafter, barbed wire and batons were the order of the day at all of the Springboks' matches. But even this was not enough to allay the fears of the rugby authorities at Timaru where, anticipating a demonstration that they would not be able to handle, the rugby authorities cancelled the South Canterbury game.

Nevertheless, against such a grim and stifling backdrop, the tourists managed to maintain their cool and played some skilful rugby. They were unbeaten in their provincial matches and went into the third and final Test at Auckland with the series delicately balanced at one win apiece. Their star player was Naas Botha, whose kicking throughout the tour was a revelation. The fair-haired fly-half finished with 129 points from eight tour appearances in New Zealand, an impressive average of just over 16 a match.

The most bizarre game of this most bizarre tour was the final Test – the series decider in Auckland. During the match a Cessna aircraft constantly strafed the pitch with flour bombs, flares and leaflets. The plane passed so low at times that there were fears that it might crash and in one of its missions the All Black prop Gary Knight was temporarily stunned by a flour bomb. But both captains insisted on referee Clive Norling of Wales allowing the game to run its course and the highest moment of rugby drama of the entire tour came in the final moments of time added on for stoppages. Allan Hewson, the New Zealand full-back, kicked a long range penalty to win the Test 25–22 and wrap up the series.

'There will probably never be another Test match like this,' wrote the New Zealand rugby historians Rod Chester and Nev McMillan. 'The tension generated by the closeness and importance of the game, combined with the efforts of protesters inside, outside and above the ground, made for an exhilarating and yet terrifying afternoon.'

THE MOST FAMOUS STREAKER OF THEM ALL

TWICKENHAM, JANUARY 1982

The streaking phenomenon began among American college students in the 1970s, but the first streaker to bare all in front of thousands at a sporting event was Michael O'Brien at Twickenham during the 1974 England-Wales rugby match. He started the craze for stripping off at big sporting occasions and was famously captured on photographic film, a Christ-like figure being frog-marched along Twickenham's east touchline by local bobby, PC Perry, who had thoughtfully removed his helmet to cover young O'Brien's embarrassment.

O'Brien, who is now a respectable stockbroker living in Australia, was swiftly removed to Twickenham police station where he was charged and released. According to legend, he managed to get back into the ground to see the last 20 minutes of England's first victory over the Welsh for 11 years.

The most famous streak and certainly the most publicised one came at the same ground during an England-Australia match nearly eight years after O'Brien's pioneering effort. Erika Roe, a 24-year-old who worked for an art dealer in Petersfield, thoughtfully waited until half-time during a tense match to make her eye-catching appearance in front of the packed south stand on a day early in the New Year. 'I didn't want to interrupt the game – I wanted to watch it,' she explained to an interviewer later.

The media had a field day. 'Titters at Twickers,' it was revealed in one tabloid, while the game's bible, the *Rothmans Rugby Yearbook*, referred to a highlight of the season being 'when a lady named Erika erupted on to the field like a galleon in full sail, but minus her spinnakers.'

But perhaps the best comment of all came from one of the England players who was temporarily distracted from the captain's pep-talk during Ms Roe's half-time interlude. Bill Beaumont was the England skipper at the time and his side were only 6–3 ahead with the wind to face after the break. The result was far from a foregone conclusion and Bill was earnestly trying to rally his troops for a big effort in the second half when he realised no-one was listening to him. 'What's the problem?' he asked. 'Everyone's watching a girl over there who seems to have your bum on her chest, Bill,' came the reply.

Erika's display inspired England to great heights in the second half as they ran out 15–11 winners.

ALPHABET SOUP

TWICKENHAM, APRIL 1983

In the early years of the game, identifying players posed a big problem for spectators. Although programmes listing teams have been part and parcel of rugby since the 1870s, jersey numbering as an aid to identification was not introduced until the early 1900s. The first international match to feature numbered teams was probably the famous Wales–New Zealand clash of 1905, though it was not until 1922, when Wales and England met at Cardiff, that both sides first wore numbers in a Five Nations game.

The Scots were the last to adopt the practice of identification, but by the 1930s it was common for teams to be labelled in all big matches. Even then, however, there was no systematic approach to the allocation of labels to positions. Some sides numbered from 1–15 starting with the full-back and working through the side to the forwards, while others started with the halves or even with the back row. In the late 1920s, Wales even refused to issue a number 13 jersey for superstitious reasons – not that they ever seemed to win during a decade of rugby disasters for the principality. They then completely and inexplicably abandoned numbers for letters in the 1930s, a practice that lasted for nearly 20 years until 1949 when a new red dye was adopted for the national shirts and they reverted to numbered jerseys.

So, the famous Welsh fly-half factory immortalised in song by Max Boyce that made 'number tens' for Wales, actually churned out Cliff Jones in the 1930s with the letter 'F' on his back and Cliff Morgan in the 1950s wearing number six. Then in 1967 the International Board legislated that the numbering of Test teams should be standardised according to a fashion that persists to this day. Therefore, David Watkins, Barry John and Phil Bennett were the first authentic fly-halves to wear the number ten shirt for Wales.

Until rugby became professional, the clubs were allowed to use whatever system took their fancies – either letters or numbers. Bath, like the old Welsh teams, numbered from 1–16 leaving out number 13, while two of England's other major clubs, Bristol and Leicester, curiously settled for letters. What made the alphabet soup even more confusing when these two sides met was the fact that Bristol lettered from A to O starting from the full-back while Leicester labelled in the reverse order. The most famous occasion on which the two clubs met in a life-sized game of Rugby Scrabble was in the John Player Cup final at Twickenham in 1983. Bristol beat Leicester 28–22 on a day when two of the best fly-halves in England, Stuart Barnes of Bristol and Les Cusworth of Leicester, wore jerseys lettered F and J respectively.

At least the professional era has ensured that English club matches are now played by teams that wear numbers that are meaningful to everyone.

A VERY PECULIAR SENDING OFF

LAUGHARNE, JANUARY 1988

Gerry 'Ginger' McLoughlin was a bulwark of the Ireland pack that won the Triple Crown and Championship in 1982. A man of tremendous strength, he provided the abiding memory of the famous win at Twickenham that year when, early in the second half, he led a raid for the corner from a maul in the English 22 and finished off scoring the only try of his Test career to set Ireland on course for a 16–15 victory.

He was a typical son of Munster, hailing from Limerick, and his shock of red hair made him stand out in even the most protracted scrum or maul. Never one to start trouble, he would be the first to admit that he was never an angel on the rugby pitch. Certainly he was well able to mix it with the best of them during a successful playing career that culminated in a Lions tour to New Zealand in 1983.

Long after his international career was over he took up a position as bar steward at the Gilfach Goch rugby club in Wales and frequently turned out for the first XV. He was a part of the side that enjoyed a run to the fourth round of the WRU Challenge Cup in 1988.

In the third round match of that campaign at Laugharne, he was involved in a very peculiar incident. An argy-bargy involving some of the front-row forwards at a line-out attracted the attention of Roy Rees, the referee. Ginger, never one to argue with authority but perhaps revealing his guilty conscience, heard the referee's comments and trudged quietly off the pitch to his early shower and thought nothing more about the incident.

Some 15 minutes or so later Mr Rees realised that Gilfach were a man short when a scrum went down minus a tight-head prop. It then dawned on everyone that Ginger had thought that he had been sent off and had left the field. Apparently, when he lectured the players for that bit of nonsense at the line-out Mr Rees had said sternly: 'Push off and let's get on with the game.' Ginger literally took 'push off' to be his marching orders.

Gilfach's 14 men won through all the same beating Laugharne 28–19.

AN ABANDONED INTERNATIONAL

COLORADO SPRINGS, JULY 1991

Although there have been several postponed Tests and even a handful of cancelled international matches down the years, there have been only two Tests that actually started but never finished.

In February 1885 at the Ormeau Grounds in Belfast, Ireland and Scotland played for 30 minutes in a storm before the match was abandoned. Scotland led by a try to nil when the sides retired and in the discussions that took place afterwards, it was decided that the score should stand unless a replay could be rearranged.

A replay was arranged and the sides met a fortnight later in Edinburgh where the Scots again held the upper hand, winning by the convincing margin of a goal and two tries to nil. At the time, the abandoned match was erased from the record books and both Unions recognised only the replayed match as having a place in the official log of the series. It was more than a hundred years later that the abandoned game was officially recognised and given retrospective Test status in both Ireland and Scotland.

The only other match to fall into the abandoned category took place during France's warm-up tour for the 1991 World Cup. They played four matches that summer in North America, including two Tests against the US Eagles. The second of the internationals, staged in Colorado Springs, started in a downpour and, when thunder and lightning came perilously close to the playing area, referee Albert Adams from South Africa abandoned the match in the interest of safety. France were leading 10–3, Serge Blanco having scored the thirty-eighth and last Test try of his illustrious career, when Mr Adams called the game off at half-time.

French minds, perhaps, went back to a tragic occasion in May 1976 when one of their talented international wings of the time, Jean-François Philiponeau, was struck by lightning and killed whilst playing in a friendly for his club, Montferrand. He was only 25 at the time.

THE WORLD CUP'S DEFINING MOMENT

CARDIFF, OCTOBER 1991

Momentum for a Rugby World Cup gathered pace during the early 1980s. Most of the drive for a world-wide tournament came from the southern hemisphere and was probably fuelled by their desire to have a formal competition that enabled the mighty Tri Nation powers to compare themselves. Less enthusiasm for the idea came from the European countries who, after all, had the Five Nations. By 1986, however, players everywhere were warming to the idea and a year later the inaugural competition was held in Australia and New Zealand.

There was no qualifying tournament for admission to that first World Cup. Sixteen nations took part by invitation and after a heady month of 32 international matches New Zealand beat France 29–9 in the first final in Auckland. The tournament was a resounding success and quickly established itself as the focal point of the game. Membership of the International Board grew apace after that and qualifying rounds and seeding tournaments were held before the 1991 event which took place in Britain, Ireland and France.

As a result of the pre-tournament matches the only newcomers in 1991 were Western Samoa. In 1990 they had finished top of the Asian-Pacific qualifying group, defeating Japan, Korea and Tonga, and were thus seeded behind Australia, Wales and Argentina in the World Cup group based in Wales. No-one expected them to win a game, even though the Samoans were sitting on a 15-match unbeaten international record that stretched back to their defeat by Romania in Bucharest two years earlier.

Their eagerly awaited opening group match was on the first Sunday of the competition against Wales at Cardiff. It was the first time that Wales played a home international on a Sunday and it was to become the first time that one of the so-called minnow nations – those who were not among the Big Eight senior members of the International Board – beat a senior nation in the World Cup.

The Western Samoans triumphed 16–13, the match turning early in the second half when To'o Vaega scored a try following up a kick ahead. That was the score that launched a golden period of Samoan offence. With 25 minutes to go the Western Samoans were 13–3 ahead and as the Welsh spectators began whistling 'Always look on the bright side of life' somehow everyone present knew that they were witnessing a piece of rugby history.

Wales did restore some pride by scoring a late try, but the result meant that only the failures of others would enable them to reach their expected quarter final. 'Good job we didn't have to play the whole of Samoa,' said a disgruntled Welsh spectator as he made his way from the ground after the match.

The Samoans gave Australia, the eventual Cup winners, a tough game in pouring rain at Pontypool before going down 9–3, but their subsequent 35–12 win against Argentina at Sardis Road, Pontypridd, assured them of a quarter-final with Scotland and eliminated Wales from the final stages.

The darlings of the competition, the Samoans were finally knocked out at Murrayfield but still managed a joyous lap of honour for their handful of followers in Edinburgh and their thousands watching on a large screen out in the open and in the middle of the night back home in Apia. But it was that defeat of Wales at Cardiff that was the defining moment of World Cup history, showing that the old order could no longer be taken for granted.

TRY FROM THE END OF THE WORLD

AUCKLAND, JULY 1994

You have to hand it to the French: for manufacturing tries out of the blue they are unsurpassable. Witness that miraculous effort from their own dead-ball-line in the 1991 Grand Slam decider against England at Twickenham. It was the longest move leading up to a try in any Test match, yet sadly for France they lost the game.

The French produced a similar effort at Auckland in the second Test of their tour of New Zealand three years later. It, too, was a surprise move launched from a do-or-die position near the French line which then swept the length of the pitch. But the difference this time was that the try, which was one of the most remarkable tries in the annals of Test rugby, won the match for France.

France had never won a Test series against the All Blacks and only four visitors in nearly a century of combat had succeeded in taking a rubber in New Zealand before Philippe Saint André's side descended on Auckland for the final match of their tour. With 90 seconds of play remaining the French trailed 20–16 as Steve Bachop, New Zealand's fly-half, attempted to push them back into their own 22 with a kick to touch. His kick missed its target but was gathered by Saint André, who with 13 of his colleagues in front of him, launched an ambitious counter-attack instead of kicking for touch.

He ran past three New Zealanders and made his way to his own 10-m line, where he was eventually overwhelmed by All Black tackles. But the damage had been done. His run had made inroads into the defence and, more importantly, put the rest of his team into a position from which the attack could be continued. The French props then did their spadework and dug the ball out from the ruck, whereupon it passed through three more pairs of hands before Emile Ntamack stretched his legs and passed the ball on to Laurent Cabannes. The flanker combined with Yann Delaigue to turn the remaining All Black defence inside out and they worked Guy Accoceberry, moving diagonally to the left, clear for a run to the posts. Showing a quick turn of pace, New Zealand's full-back John Timu came speeding across to take the Frenchman, but Jean-Luc Sadourny had by now raced up outside Accoceberry and he was on hand to take the pass and slide over to the left of the posts for the try that won the match and with it the series.

'It was a try from the end of the world,' said a delighted and exhausted Saint André at the post match press conference. Everyone knew what he meant. It was the most sensational last-minute winning try in France's Test history to date.

LIGHTS GO OUT IN PORT ELIZABETH

PORT ELIZABETH, JUNE 1995

The Boet Erasmus Stadium in Port Elizabeth has had its share of difficult moments in its Test history. In 1963, in the final Test of that year's series between the Springboks and the Wallabies, the match erupted into a riot in the second half as bottles were thrown on to the pitch, cars were vandalised and policemen had to fire pistols into the air to quell demonstrators. The Australians, who understandably were more concerned for their own safety than with the play of the Springboks, wanted the referee to abandon the match. 'It was a complete shambles,' one of the Australian players was reported to have said, reflecting on the failure of officials to keep the crowd under control.

Thirty-two years later, during the Rugby World Cup, the Boet Erasmus administration had more nightmares, this time as a result of power failure. South Africa and Canada were due to meet one another at the ground in a pool match, but a floodlight failure delayed the start of the match by 40 minutes. But by the end of the match, it was rugby football itself that plunged into darkness. A highly unsavoury incident late in the match was witnessed by millions of viewers around the world. Ten minutes from time a scuffle began near the touchline and turned into a huge brawl as several players from both sides became involved with fists and feet flying. It ended in the sending off of three players – two Canadians, Gareth Rees and Rod Snow, plus the

Springboks' hooker, James Dalton. Dalton thus missed the opportunity to play in the knockout stages that took his side to the final of the competition, as too did the winger Pieter Hendriks, who although not sent off at the time, was later cited for his part in the fracas and suspended accordingly.

The strange upshot was that South Africa were permitted to replace the players suspended from the squad, enabling them to introduce their ace three-quarter Chester Williams, who had been unavailable through injury when the original squad for the competition had been named three weeks earlier.

GREEN VOLVO STOPS PLAY

SUNBURY, MARCH 1996

The current hum that surrounds the London Irish club dates from 1996 when, as a second division side, two strong personalities, Clive Woodward the coach and Gary Halpin the captain, stamped their mark on a team that began to play expansive rugby. Strong running backs and competitive forwards provided the momentum that drove the club to the top of the table and promotion to the top flight of English rugby.

The 1995–6 season was also memorable as it saw London Irish's best Cup run since their appearance in the 1980 final when they were beaten by Leicester. The Tigers were again their opponents at Sunbury in March 1996 when the clubs were drawn to meet in the semi-finals.

A capacity crowd was in attendance to set both a gate record and a Guinness consumption record for the club. London Irish boldly set out to play their wide game, making no concessions to the forward power of the renowned Leicester forwards. Although the Tigers were ahead 22–8 after only 27 minutes, the storming play of Rob Henderson and the effective goal kicking of Michael Corcoran brought the Irish back into the game and by the interval they only trailed by the slim margin of one point with the score at 21–22.

Then, five minutes into the second half, the concentration of the London Irish team was broken by an event that could only have happened at London Irish. So many had turned up at the ground to watch the match that parking arrangements had been chaotic right up to the time of the kick-off with cars being parked anywhere and everywhere. As the referee prepared to restart the game with a scrum after a break in play, the public announcement system rumbled into action to request that the owner of a green Volvo, registration number … , remove it immediately otherwise the police would do so.

As the scrum was about to go down, Gary Halpin, at tight head prop, held the front rows up. The tannoy message had suddenly sunk in: that green Volvo belonged to none other than the London Irish skipper himself. Play had to be held up while he ambled across the pitch to the dressing room, where he recovered his car keys and gave them to a friend so that the car could be moved.

Unfortunately, the poor Irish never recovered after that, and Leicester raced 46–21 ahead and into a Cup final against Bath.

CROSS CODE CHALLENGE

TWICKENHAM, MAY 1996

A meeting of the Rugby Football Union (RFU) on 19 September 1895 outlawed professionalism in any form and adopted strict new by-laws to govern the structure of the amateur rugby union game. These laws were framed as a reaction to a number of clubs in the north of England who had met two months earlier to vote for a breakaway and formation of what was then known as the Northern Union and which became the rugby league. The main plank of the newly formed organisation's constitution was that a six shilling (30 pence) broken time payment would be made to compensate players for loss of employment, something which the die-hards of the RFU could not and would not entertain.

The two games went strictly down their own paths for a century except during war-time. On the 14 November 1939, the RFU temporarily lifted the ban so that rugby league and rugby union players could join arms to play in service matches until official matches began again in peacetime. Interestingly, the Scottish Union saw no reason for removing the bar on league men.

There were two cross code challenges during the war, the League XV winning the first match 18–11 at Headingley in January 1943. A year later, in April 1944, another special match arranged by Northern Command in which a Rugby League Selection played a Rugby Union Selection was staged at the league's stronghold, Odsal Stadium in Bradford. The match, again played under the 15-a-side code, attracted more than 18,000 curious spectators and raised over £1,350 for charity. As expected, the strong Union XV went ahead early on and led 10–0 at the interval. The League outfit, however, staged a remarkable comeback in the second half and ran out deserved winners by 15–10.

But it was not until rugby union went open in September 1995 with the introduction of the seamless game that the drawbridge between the two codes permanently came down. To celebrate the end of the 100 years' war between league and union, a pair of interesting and unusual challenge matches involving Bath, the English rugby union champions, and Wigan, their rugby league counterparts, were enacted.

The first leg of the challenge, under rugby league rules, was at Maine Road, Manchester early in May 1996. Former Welsh rugby union international and distinguished league coach, Clive Griffiths, was drafted in to give the Bath boys a crash course in the subtleties of the 13-a-side game. A trial match against the South Wales League XIII was a useful taster for the Union boys who did well to score four tries despite conceding eight.

Then it was up to Manchester for the match against the side that had been the cream of the league game for several years. What Bath had done for modern English club rugby union, Wigan had done for rugby league.

Of course, Bath were smashed to smithereens in what amounted to a massive culture shock. It was 82–6 at the end, Wigan strolling in for 16 tries to one scored by Jon Callard. Wigan's lines of running, superior basic skills and imaginative use of space left a deep impression on the Bath players. 'Wigan are a fantastic side,' said Bath captain Phil de Glanville, reflecting on the pace, power and superior fitness of his opponents after the match. 'We turned up,' was the final word of the Bath director of rugby, John Hall.

When Wigan met Bath in the return match, this time under union rules at Twickenham, the kings of the north had already paraded their skills at the ground as special guests of the organising committee of the annual Middlesex Sevens. The Sevens tournament was the first time that a rugby league side had set foot on the hallowed turf of RFU headquarters, something that could not possibly have been envisaged even five years earlier. Wigan again displayed their sublime skills and entertained a hugely appreciative crowd, beating Harlequins and Leicester before winning the final against Wasps.

Honour at least was restored in the 15-a-side part of the cross code challenge with Bath winning the Twickenham match by 44–19. Even so, Wigan certainly threw down the gauntlet to the English Union champions. It was felt that they would struggle in the scrums, line-outs and rucks, but bolstered by former exponents of the Union game such as Scott Quinnell, Martin Offiah (who had scored six tries at Maine Road) and Inga Tuigamala (who began the match as a flanker), and to a lesser extent, by some sympathetic refereeing from Brian Campsall, the northern champions managed three sparkling tries.

ENGLAND'S WORST HALF-HOUR

TWICKENHAM, MARCH 1997

English supporters had never seen anything like the last 30 minutes of the Twickenham Five Nations match against France on St David's Day, 1997 – not in 129 years covering 475 international matches since 1871.

England, after conceding an early penalty goal in the third minute of the match, were up and in the faces of the French almost from the word go. For the first hour the forwards joined the backs in the 15-man game that coach Jack Rowell preferred to call inter-active rugby as England swept all before them.

The boot of Paul Grayson put England ahead in the first half. The Northampton fly-half kicked three penalties to give them a 9–3 advantage after only a dozen minutes and though Christophe Lamaison pulled back three points with a dropped goal for France, Lawrence Dallaglio scored with a 30-m dash on the stroke of half-time. That score, England's high moment of the match, stretched England into a 14–6 lead that became 20–6 after two more Paul Grayson penalties in the first ten minutes of the second half. 'Swing Low' sang the crowd, anticipating more momentum being generated by its sweet chariot.

But in the last 30 minutes of this vivid match the chariot ground to a halt and eventually lost its wheels. In quite the most extraordinary turn-round ever seen in an England international, Phil de Glanville's men lost the initiative to a

French side that began to play with dash. Lamaison was the spark in the backs. Running at the English three-quarters, the Frenchman looked positively dangerous every time he gained possession. Flanker Olivier Magne played with a panache reminiscent of the great Jean-Pierre Rives and was the catalyst in the move that led to France's first try 20 minutes from the end. As play moved to the right the ball came to Lamaison, who dropped a delicate chip into the path of Laurent Leflammand, who gathered it one-handed and swerved outside Tony Underwood for a corner score. Lamaison converted from a difficult angle.

Seven minutes later it was Lamaison who again stormed England's defences after a series of clever French blind-side attacks. His conversion of his own try brought his side level with ten minutes remaining. Then, to cap it all, he kicked the winning penalty three minutes from time making the scoreline 23–20 to France who had scored 17 points without reply while Lamaison had registered the full house of scoring actions: try, conversions and penalties to add to his earlier dropped goal. England had never previously surrendered such a commanding lead.

SIXTY TEST POINTS SCORED AT THE SAME END

DUNEDIN, AUGUST 1997

The Tri Nations tournament launched in 1996 derived from the negotiations that South African, New Zealand and Australian rugby representatives had with Rupert Murdoch's NewsCorp television executives at the time of the 1995 Rugby World Cup. In return for £360 million, the three southern hemisphere powers confirmed that they would meet one another home and away on a round-robin basis every season for the following decade, with Murdoch's media interests having sole broadcasting rights to the competition.

The tournament was an instant success. At last the southern powers had a competition to rival the long established European Five Nations, and crowds flocked to see New Zealand walk off with the inaugural title. In winning the 1996 title, the All Blacks had carried off a Grand Slam and were thus seeking back-to-back Grand Slams when, in the following year's competition, they hosted Australia at Dunedin's Carisbrook ground in mid-August.

New Zealand were unstoppable and powered into an unassailable 36–0 lead in the first 40 minutes. They ran in three tries through Taine Randell, Justin Marshall and Christian Cullen and, with Carlos Spencer in deadly form with the boot, everyone thought that the game was over by the interval. Everyone, that is, except the Australian team.

The Wallabies turned round to stage a spirited recovery

in a fascinating second half that was partially spoilt by a number of interruptions for penalties. (All told, French official Joel Dumé saw fit to award 38 penalties during the match.) Stephen Larkham (twice), Joe Roff and Ben Tune ripped the New Zealand defence open to cross for tries, but David Knox managed only two conversions to leave the Wallabies still a dozen points short of the All Blacks, despite outscoring them on tries.

The final result was 36–24 to New Zealand but the scoreline provided the statisticians with the oddity that all 60 of the points gained in the Test match had been registered at the same end of the ground.

FASTEST TEST TRY

MURRAYFIELD, FEBRUARY 1999

In 1923 at Twickenham, Wales had conceded the then fastest try scored in Test history when Leo Price touched down for England ten seconds after the kick-off. The record that no-one believed could be beaten stood for more than 76 years until Wales, again, conceded an even quicker one at Murrayfield on the opening day of the last ever Five Nations tournament.

Duncan Hodge lined up as if to take an orthodox kick-off for Scotland with his forwards in scrum formation to his right. As the referee blew his whistle to signal the start of the match, Hodge switched direction and angled the ball to the less densely populated left where only Matthew Robinson and Shane Howarth were in position for Wales. Howarth moved ahead of Robinson to claim the kick but had not anticipated the quick reactions of the Scottish left-centre, John Leslie. Leslie, the son of a former All Blacks captain, swooped for the ball like a bat out of hell and snatched it from Howarth's grasp and set off on a run towards the Welsh line. On and on he sprinted as the Welsh cover, badly caught on the hop, desperately tried to cut across and atone for its poor organisation at the kick-off. Leslie loped into the Welsh 22 and finished off crashing over to the left of the posts.

Most of the sell-out crowd had barely settled in their seats and Scotland were already five points ahead. In the press box, journalists frantically looked at their stop watches to clock Leslie's time. Eight seconds? Nine, ten, eleven ... It wasn't really until the BBC had rerun the score several times at the interval that an accurate fix could be made on the score. The media boys reckoned it had taken Leslie nine seconds to score, clipping Leo Price's run-in by one second and setting a new world record for an international match – one that is never likely to be beaten.

The start of the game set the tempo for the following 79 minutes and 50 seconds. Points came thick and fast before Scotland finished 33–20 winners of a match that yielded six tries. Afterwards, Leslie modestly acknowledged the part played in his try by the rest of the Scottish side. 'We planned to put Matthew Robinson under pressure right from the kick off,' he said, 'so although it was a quick try, it was something we had been working on.'

UPSET OF THE MILLENNIUM

TWICKENHAM, OCTOBER 1999

The northern hemisphere's last rugby season of the millennium generated more surprise Test results than any other in the game's history. There was Italy's astonishing debut in the Six Nations when they beat Scotland, the reigning Five Nations champions, and Ireland ended the longest series of defeats in any Test rugby series when they triumphed against France in Paris for the first time in 28 years. But the match that stands out as the surprise of the season is the New Zealand–France semi-final staged at Twickenham in the Rugby World Cup tournament earlier in the season.

The French had struggled against Canada and Fiji to win their pool games before beating Argentina in a quarter final at Lansdowne Road in Dublin. All roads led to Twickenham for the semis, where Australia disposed of South Africa on the Saturday of a delicious weekend of double headers at the Rugby Football Union's headquarters. Sunday's second semi-final, between New Zealand and France, was considered such a formality that many French supporters didn't even bother to make the visit to London to see their side in action.

After all, only four months earlier in Wellington, the French had been overwhelmed 54–7 by the All Blacks during a tour that was meant to act as a build-up to the World Cup tournament. No, France definitely didn't have a chance in the semi-finals and the French press proclaimed as much, too.

The early stages of the match seemed to support all the pre-match expectations that New Zealand would coast into the finals. The All Blacks efficiently compiled a 17–10 lead by half-time and went further ahead through a Jonah Lomu try converted by Andrew Mehrtens four minutes after the interval: 24–10 to New Zealand with 35 minutes to go, it was all over bar the shouting – or so everyone thought.

Then came the most extraordinary rearguard action of the millennium. Christophe Lamaison started the French ball rolling with a couple of neatly executed dropped goals in the sixth and ninth minutes of the second half and suddenly the game took on a different complexion. The French front row were holding up their much vaunted rivals, the French line-out with Abdel Benazzi in commanding form was ruling the set-pieces, and their backs, with nothing to lose now, scented the outside chance of upsetting their famous counterparts.

The French spirit was epitomised by the smallest man on the field, the left wing Christophe Dominici from the Paris club, Stade Français. His mad-cap runs at the New Zealand defence paid the unlikeliest dividends. He turned the All Black defence inside out with his mazy runs and gave inspiration to the other 14 men in blue. Two Lamaison penalties brought the French back to within two points of the All Blacks before, on the quarter hour, Dominici himself scorched over for the try that put France ahead. With their handful of supporters and virtually all of the thousands of neutral spectators firmly behind them, the French lead was one that they would not relinquish. Richard Dourthe and Philippe Bernat-Salles finished off glorious French attacks with tries that Lamaison converted to bring him a personal tally of 28 points in the match and, with seven minutes to go, the most extraordinary of Test transformations had taken the score from 10–24 in New Zealand's favour to 43–24 to France.

Never before had the All Blacks conceded 33 points without reply and certainly never before had they given away 43 points in a Test. The textbook approach of the New Zealanders, with the emphasis on eliminating errors and pressurising opponents until gaps opened up had, in one wonderful half-hour, been superseded by the brilliantly unpredictable approach adopted by the French, who played the games of their lives to win with a display of passion and flair.

For the All Blacks, defeat was hard to bear. Their highly respected coach, John Hart, announced his resignation and an entire nation went into mourning. The defeat was even cited as the root cause of the ruling New Zealand Government's fall at the General Election that took place shortly after the end of the Rugby World Cup.

EUROPEAN FIASCO

LLANELLI, APRIL 2000

It was billed as the most important Welsh club match of all time. Llanelli versus Cardiff at Stradey Park in the quarter-final of the Heineken European Cup.

The match turned into a yawn. A dull game ensued with virtually no passages of back play for the sell-out crowd to savour. Llanelli went through to the semi-finals comfortably, but at a time when senior rugby needed the oxygen of good publicity for its increasingly important new competition, once again an opportunity for promoting the game was spoiled by inefficient administrators.

Mid-way through the first-half the referee Didier Mené of France, who had experienced a difficult time quelling the tempers of two charged-up packs, sent loose forwards Owain Williams (Cardiff) and Ian Boobyer (Llanelli) to the sin-bin after a dust-up. Quite right, too, thought the sizeable audience watching the match on BBC television. After all, only an hour earlier in the other European quarter-final being played that day, Stade Français's New Zealand-born centre, Cliff Mytton, had been dealt similar justice playing against Munster by referee Steve Lander.

The two Welsh forwards had been off the field for five minutes when a fiasco began. There was a break in play during which Monsieur Mené's attention was caught by fourth official Ken Brackston and one of the Heineken tournament's organisers.

The Frenchman was informed that there was no sin-bin in operation in the European competitions and that, while the yellow cards shown to Williams and Boobyer should stand, the players should be reinstated immediately. So, after only five minutes off the field, the two forwards rejoined the fray and the match continued its otherwise uneventful course to half-time.

It was during the interval that the farce reached Brian Rix proportions. What about the events over in Munster barely an hour earlier? Munster had piled on nine points during Mytton's absence. If, as now seemed likely, the sin-bin did not apply to the tournament, what would be Stade Français's reaction? Would they demand a replay?

Frantic telephone calls were made to Roger Pickering, head honcho of the European Rugby Committee that oversees the Heineken tournament. He at last cleared up the misunderstandings. In January, it transpired, the European Rugby Committee had taken on board the International Board's recommendations regarding use of the sin-bin. The quarter-finals of the Cup were the first Euro matches to be staged since those guidelines had been issued. Unfortunately, a lack of communication had meant that clubs, referees and tournament organisers were unsure of the yellow-card and sin-bin procedure.

Fortunately, the misunderstanding had no bearing on the outcome of the match. For good measure, Monsieur Mené sent Cardiff flanker Martyn Williams to the sin-bin for the full ten minutes after a second-half offence, but the whole affair did little to inspire public confidence in those who administer professional rugby.

RYAN'S SIX THE BEST

BEDFORD, APRIL 2000

Bedford were the whipping boys of the Allied Dunbar Premiership in 1999–2000. Their first win of the season did not come until April, when they defeated Harlequins, but a week later they were brought back to earth by a Saracens team in which Ryan Constable set a record.

Constable, a former Australian cap, returned from duty with the Aussie Sevens side to play in the Sunday match at Goldington Road. The game also marked Kyran Bracken's first senior start after a long period out of rugby through injury.

Constable was the main beneficiary of Bracken's slick service from the base of the scrum. The Sarries backs ran their hapless opponents into the ground and by half-time the Australian three-quarter had already scored a hat-trick of tries as his side ran up a 35–12 lead.

After the break Constable advanced to his record, becoming the first player in League history to score six tries in a first division match with a hat trick in both halves. His tries helped his club to a 57–29 win, though the record-breaker was modest in his post-match summing up. 'I was just on the end of some good lead-up work,' he told the *Watford Observer*'s rugby reporter after the match.

The previous record was five tries set by Kenny Logan while playing for Wasps.

FIFTEEN MINUTES OF FAME

BUCHAREST, APRIL 2000

The Dorchester Gladiators enjoyed their 15 minutes of rugby fame on an Easter tour of Romania in 2000. The occasional team of rugby enthusiasts were visiting Bucharest to distribute toys to an orphanage when, thanks to the intervention of a kindly embassy official, they were invited to play a rugby match against one of the Romanian clubs. The Dorchester party, comprising a lively but unfit group of forty-somethings, jumped at the opportunity of playing what they imagined would be a social match against the locals, with the chance to down a couple of pints of Romanian best afterwards.

Unfortunately, an error in translation led to the Romanians greatly overestimating the quality of their English opponents. As a result, the Dorchester boys arrived for their 11a.m. kick-off only to find that the venue was the National Stadium, that an expectant crowd of thousands had turned up and that the match was to be broadcast live on Romanian television. Their opponents, moreover, were Romania's crack club side, Steaua Bucharest. The hosts fielded half-a-dozen full international players as well as the captain of the Romanian national side.

'We were a bit suspicious when the hosts offered us a training session the night before,' said lock forward Nigel Jones on the Gladiator's return. 'Not exactly our style,' he continued, 'we did our pre-match build-up in the bar.'

The Romanians, perhaps confusing the name Gladiators with Saracens or the Barbarians, believed their visitors were packed with England's top professional players, despite attempts from the Dorchester players to explain otherwise.

It was only on the pitch that the truth began to dawn on the Romanians. 'They warmed up like professionals while we stood around smoking cigarettes, knowing we were in for trouble,' one of the Gladiators revealed. Once the match started, Steaua quickly piled on the points before realising that they were involved in a mis-match. Consequently, the hosts eased up for the second half and the final score was 60–17.

The Gladiators' full-back, Dave Scaddon, told reporters: 'They were incredibly fit and all in their twenties. People kept telling us they thought we had done brilliantly under the circumstances.'

A HELPING HAND

LONDON, OCTOBER 2000

Diego Dominguez was one of the most prolific points scorers in the history of the game. Between 1989 and 2003 he amassed the staggering total of 1010 points in international matches, becoming only the second player to date to pass a thousand at this level. Born in Córdoba, Argentina, he played twice for the Pumas in the 1989 South American Championship before moving to Milan where, between 1990 and 1997 he scored 2,966 points in Serie A rugby. From 1991 to 2003 he was Italy's first-choice outside-half and his kicking steered the azzurri to their famous 34-20 victory over Scotland when Italy joined the Six Nations in 2000.

In 1997, a couple of years into the game's professional era, he switched allegiance to the resurgent Stade Français club in Paris and by 2000 was a key member of the side's assault on Europe. It was in the Heineken Cup, Europe's premier sub-international tournament, that the most unusual three points of his career were scored.

Stade were visiting Wasps for the fourth round of the Cup's pool stages. Stade had lost once and Wasps twice, and Stade had overcome Wasps at home in the previous round. A win would keep alive either side's hopes; defeat would almost certainly end them.

Conditions in London were appalling. Heavy rain wrecked the match as a spectacle and the sides had to rely on their kickers as their main sources of points. With 12 minutes to go to the end, Stade led 28–21 when Dominguez stepped up to take another kick at goal.

Earlier he had converted the only try of the match scored and landed seven penalties from seven attempts – a remarkable achievement given the wet conditions. This eighth penalty attempt was from half-way.

The attempt appeared to be on target but the swirling wind was clearly bringing the ball down short of the crossbar. As the ball dipped Richard Birkett, Wasps' 6ft 4in (1.93m) replacement flanker, was lifted by his team-mates in an attempt to catch the ball. But the jump was slightly mis-timed and, to everyone's amazement, the ball glanced off the top of Birkett's hands, up and over the crossbar. His helping hand had given Dominguez his twenty-eighth point of the match, Stade went 31–21 ahead, and with Wasps responding with a late converted try to make it 31–28, the unusual penalty was the difference between the sides at the end of the match.

David Hands, the most respected rugby critic on rugby union's media circuit with more than 30 years reporting the game at the highest level, told readers of *The Times* that the incident 'may be unique … in the first class game.'

The only comparable event occurred a few years earlier when John Eales jumped high for the Queensland Reds to catch an Auckland penalty attempt in a Super 12 match. On that occasion Eales intercepted the kick, knocking the ball forward to concede a scrum. The Queensland coach that day was John Connolly, who by coincidence was Stade's coach in 2000. But even he had never seen an 'assist' before.

GLOUCESTER'S DROP OF LUCK

GLOUCESTER, JANUARY 2001

One of the key matches in the 2000-01 Heineken Cup occurred in the penultimate round of pool matches in January 2001 when Gloucester entertained Llanelli. The match took on the feel of a knockout game because victory for either side virtually guaranteed finishing at the head of their pool ensuring qualification for the quarter-finals.

For that reason the game was played like a knockout game. It was hugely enjoyable to watch, Llanelli's spirit of adventure contrasting sharply with Gloucester's usual brave but limited approach. The game was scrappy, but after 77 minutes Llanelli led 27–25 and all concerned felt that, with time running out, justice would be done. The Scarlet runners had produced two trademark tries for fleet-footed Mark Jones, and they were only denied a third try when prop Martyn Madden just failed to gather a pass from lock Vernon Cooper.

Gloucester's game plan appeared to be to keep possession and force play deep enough into Llanelli territory for Simon Mannix to pop over penalty goals. The plan had been successful. The former New Zealand first five-eighth had landed five penalties and converted Gloucester's only try to keep his side in touch.

Then with two minutes to go, Gloucester's Elton Moncreiff thought he could win the match when he attempted a drop at goal. The ball barely reached shoulder level and most thought that Gloucester's chances of victory had vanished. But his low, scudding kick struck the shoulder of Phil Booth, Llanelli's prop, whereupon it ballooned freakishly up and over the crossbar for arguably the flukiest drop goal in Heineken Cup history.

It was Gloucester's first drop of luck of the season, the 28–27 win sending them through to the knockout stages of the competition for the first time.

OUR DEFENCE IS THEIR ENEMY

LIMERICK, JANUARY 2003

The Heineken Cup has given rugby in Ireland a tremendous shot in the arm. The Irish have regularly been represented in the competition by the famous old provinces of Munster, Ulster and Leinster, regions whose rugby traditions date back to the 1870s, and have regularly featured well beyond the pool stages.

For Munster, in particular, the Heineken Cup experience has been an epic tale in their history. Indeed from 1996, the inaugural year of European competition, until January 2007, they were unbeaten in the Cup at their Thomond Park ground in Limerick.

Even so, the province was by no means certain of qualifying for the tournament's knockout stages in 2002–03 when Gloucester pitched up for the final match of the pool stages in January. Munster had to win by a comfortable margin to ensure a place in the quarter-finals.

They finally did so with a 33–6 victory, but a wonderful story emerged a few days after the match. A Limerick taxi driver told the Irish radio station RTE that he had found a piece of paper in his cab the day before the big match. To his astonishment it turned out to be a document that detailed Gloucester's game plan for beating Munster.

The tactics, clearly addressed to the Gloucester team members, described how Ronan O'Gara, Munster's key player behind the scrum, should be targeted, it set out the line-out calls and, with typical Gloucester pragmatism concluded: 'our defence is their enemy.'

The cabbie realised its value and delivered it to the RTE offices where Pat Whelan, the former Ireland hooker, worked. Whelan immediately passed the plans to the Munster team and the rest, as they say, was history.

That the document existed and was probably genuine was confirmed by the then Gloucester coach, Nigel Melville. He said that the plans had been run off the night before the match and placed under the doors of the rooms in the Limerick hotel where the Gloucester players were staying. Quite how they came to be in the driver's possession was never really established.

Pat Geraghty, Munster's press officer, confirmed that the plans had reached the team on the morning of the match, but had not influenced the province's own tactics, which by that late stage of preparation had already been rehearsed.

The taxi driver, who maintained his anonymity throughout the episode, hoped that Munster would provide him with complimentary tickets for their Celtic Cup final in Cardiff the following weekend.

SHADES OF THE COLD WAR

KRASNODAR, MARCH 2004

One of the most peculiar drug cases that the International Rugby Board was ever asked to investigate occurred in March 2004 when Russia defeated Romania 33–24 in a European Nations Cup match. (This tournament is a shadow Six Nations tournament, though as yet there are no plans to operate promotions and relegations between Europe's elite and second-tier nations.)

Several of the players had reported feelings of drowsiness at the time of the match, but these were put down to the inhospitable travelling conditions encountered on the long overland haul around the Black Sea. Romania had been favourites to win, but suspicions regarding the Russian victory emerged when the losers returned to Bucharest on the Sunday after the match.

The Romanian Federation tested the urine of their players and discovered traces of phenothiazine, a drug that is used to sedate patients with psychotic symptoms. This led to speculation that tactics normally associated with espionage and the Cold War were used by the Russians to win a rugby match.

THREE OF A KIND

MURRAYFIELD, FEBRUARY 2007

'What a start!' is a part of Cliff Morgan's commentary on the unforgettable try scored by Gareth Edwards for the Barbarians against the All Blacks at Cardiff in 1973. It was near the beginning of a pulsating match that developed into one of the best in rugby's history.

Several other games, arguably, come into the frame for the title 'most sensational start to a match.' There was John Leslie's score for Scotland against Wales from the kick-off at Murrayfield in 1999 (described in the *Fastest Test Try*, page 208), or Brian Price's punch-up with Noel Murphy in the 1969 Triple Crown decider in Cardiff, or more recently the New Zealand–Australia Tri Nations match at Sydney in 2000 when the All Blacks scored three tries in the opening five minutes. Somehow, the fact it was New Zealand who scored the three quick tries didn't make that such a big deal.

But when Italy emulated the All Blacks' feat in a Six Nations encounter in 2007 that really was something to celebrate. The Italians had opened their campaign with defeats to France and England and, in their eighth season in the Six Nations had yet to register an away win in the tournament.

That was all to change at Murrayfield. The Italians, coached by the former French scrum-half Pierre Berbizier, had made England work hard for a 20–7 win at Twickenham a fortnight earlier and were confident of giving the Scots a stern examination. The Scots, for their part, were riding the crest of a wave having recently defeated Wales to bring up five wins in their last six internationals at home.

But not even the most optimistic of Italian fans could have envisaged their side racing away to break new ground in such dramatic circumstances. After one minute and 14 seconds Mirco Bergamasco charged down an attempted chip ahead by Phil Godman. He regathered the ball and sped away for the opening try of the match.

Barely two minutes later scrum-half Chris Cusiter telegraphed his intention to pass from a defensive ruck just outside Scotland's 22 and Andrea Scanavacca intercepted and showed the Scots a clean pair of heels.

Cusiter was embarrassed again two minutes later when another of his wayward cut-out passes gifted a try to right-wing Kaine Robertson. The speedster had to run from half-way to score, but with Scotland's defence on the back foot he crossed unchallenged. Scanavacca, with three kicks from in front of the posts, added the goal points each time.

So, a hat-trick of interception tries: three of a kind to achieve a 21-0 lead in five minutes, a feat only previously achieved by the All Blacks in an international match.

PLAYED BY YOUTHS AND WATCHED BY HOOLIGANS

GLOUCESTER, MARCH 2007

Anyone who has regularly refereed schoolboy or youth rugby will know that it can be a rewarding and enjoyable experience. Youngsters invariably play with the joy and sporting spirit that the game was probably originally intended to engender, the nefarious tricks that players learn with age and experience being noticeably absent.

The occasional and most difficult problem that faces teachers refereeing at junior level is the unacceptable behaviour of a small minority of touchline followers – usually parents – who choose the occasion to criticise decisions or, worse, vent their verbal abuse on visiting supporters – games played by youths and watched by hooligans.

Schools have, in the past, been known to break off fixtures as the result of unpleasant behaviour on the touchlines, but it has been extremely rare for disagreements to deteriorate to such an extent that youth matches have become crime scenes.

In late March, 2007, however, that is exactly what happened at Churchdown on the outskirts of Gloucester. Chosen Hill RFC's Under-16s were playing at home in a county cup semi-final. Referee Phil Harrison was in good control of the match on the pitch and later told reporters, 'It was superb rugby. The game was excellent with no violence.'

But on the sidelines an exchange of unpleasant verbal

abuse began when a parent belonging to the home club directed a remark at the mother of a visiting player from Bristol. The abuse built until it finally escalated into violence, with nearly two-dozen joining in a scrap after Chosen Hill had won the match. Innocent bystanders said that it set a terrible example to the young players.

Several involved in the fracas required treatment for cuts and bruises at Gloucestershire Royal Hospital and police confirmed that one patient was admitted with quite serious facial injuries. A spokesman for Gloucestershire Constabulary added that a 43-year-old from Churchdown was arrested on suspicion of assault and that statements were being taken to judge whether more arrests could follow if further offenders were identified.

BLOODGATE

THE TWICKENHAM STOOP, APRIL 2009

It was the scandal that rocked English rugby. A joke-shop blood capsule, a faked injury and a clumsy attempt at a cover-up were the strands of a plot that sounded so far-fetched that it couldn't have been invented.

Harlequins were playing Leinster in a Heineken Cup quarter-final at the Twickenham Stoop Ground and trailing 6–5 as the game entered its dying moments. With a semi-final place in Europe's premier club tournament the prize for the winners, the stakes were high.

Quins had scored the only try of the game through their full-back, Mike Brown, but Leinster had edged ahead through two Felipe Contepomi penalties. It had been a hard match in which both Nick Easter (Harlequins) and Contepomi had been yellow-carded and sent to the sin-bin.

Nick Evans, the former All Black fly-half and Harlequins' ace kicker, had been substituted by Chris Malone early in the second-half. Evans had been niggled by a knee ligament injury for most of the season but this was a tactical substitution. When Malone was injured ten minutes from time, Tom Williams was sent on leaving Harlequins with no recognised goal-kicker. With time running out, it seemed that Quins' only hope of victory was to score a try against one of the best defences in Europe. It didn't look likely.

With three minutes to go, Tom Williams drew the referee's attention to an apparent facial wound. Williams could be seen bleeding profusely from his mouth and was duly led off. Now whereas a substituted player cannot normally return to the field of play, Law 3.12 makes an exception for a player who is bleeding or has an open wound. Harlequins were thus able to bring Nick Evans back into the fray for a possible late dropped-goal or penalty attempt. Although Evans was clearly in discomfort and limping, Leinster officials were bristling with indignation at what they suspected was a deliberate flouting of rugby's conventions of fair play. At least justice was seen to be done when Leinster managed to retain their slender lead to win the match.

When the investigations began after the sides had left the field, a more sinister tale of deceit unravelled. Leinster protested. Their team doctor, Professor Arthur Tanner, demanded to see the extent of the Williams injury immediately, but was locked out of the treatment room. A distinguished surgeon, he felt that the bleeding looked unnatural. Williams, it was reported, required stitches in the treatment room, but rumours later spread that they were applied to a wound that had been inflicted by a member of the Harlequins back-up staff. (It later emerged that a cut had been made to make the original 'injury' look authentic.)

Suspicions that the injury had been faked were so rife that the European Rugby Cup (ERC) body responsible for the competition, quickly launched an investigation. Unseen television camera footage revealed that just before attracting the referee's attention to his injury Williams had taken advantage of a break in play, bent over and pushed his hand into one of his socks. He was seen to remove a capsule and transfer it to his mouth whereupon, moments later, blood appeared on his face. Moreover, as he went off, one camera clearly showed him winking.

ERC, after convening its independent appeal committee, were cunning in their initial judgement made in July. Their statement, based only on the evidence they had seen, banned Williams for one year for faking an injury using a theatrical blood capsule and imposed on the Harlequins a fine of 250,000 euros, 50 per cent of which was suspended for two years. They also declared that misconduct complaints against Dean Richards, the Harlequins director of rugby, Steph Brennan, the club's physio and Dr Wendy Chapman, the club doctor could not be proven. But many felt that the simplicity of ERC's ruling would fuel further recriminations.

They certainly did. The Professional Rugby Players' Association sprang to their man's defence and Tom Williams, who was of previously unquestionable character, appealed against his ban. Roger O'Connor, ERC's disciplinary officer, also appealed the dismissal of the complaints against the three Harlequins officials and the financial penalty imposed on the club, arguing for heavier punishments.

The charade was eventually exposed as a premeditated attempt to cheat. A month later ERC heard new evidence submitted by Williams, who had allegedly been offered a financial incentive by Harlequins to keep his silence. Williams admitted his part in the incident to ERC and described the steps taken to cover up what had taken place shortly after the match finished, implicating both Richards and Brennan, who both admitted their part in fabricating the blood injury using red dye.

Williams was seen as the mere fall-guy and had his ban reduced to four months, but Dean Richards, the much-respected former England number eight, was banned from rugby worldwide for three years while Steph Brennan was suspended for two. The club, which also admitted that it had considered making blood simulations in competitions outside the European tournaments on four previous occasions, had its fine increased to 300,000 euros.

The appeal against Dr Chapman, who allegedly applied the post-match cut to Williams's lip (under duress and at the player's request), was dismissed by ERC, but she was subsequently suspended on full pay by the General Medical Council pending their own investigation.

PENALTY SHOOT-OUT

CARDIFF, MAY 2009

Rugby followers had never seen anything like it before – a penalty shoot-out on British soil to decide an important match. Drawn matches are pretty rare in rugby: in the 16 seasons since the Six Nations began, for instance, there have been only five draws in 240 matches. Extra time is even rarer in rugby. It's true that a couple of high-profile World Cup games went into extra time, notably the 1995 Final when Joel Stransky's late dropped goal brought the Rainbow Nation victory; while none will ever forget Jonny Wilkinson's late dropped goal to bring England the World Cup deep into added time in the 2003 Final. But for a drawn match to then finish drawn after extra time, and with both sides level on tries, was unheard of on British or Irish soil.

There had been a Heineken Cup semi-final between Brive and Toulouse in 1998 that ended in a stalemate on points after extra time. But on that occasion Brive were awarded the verdict on superior tries scored.

Indeed, there seemed to be only one precedent worldwide for an extension of extra time in a major rugby match. The 1984 French Championship final between Béziers and Agen was decided on penalties after the match finished all-square at 12-all in 80 minutes and the sides were still deadlocked, at 21-all with identical scoring actions, at the end of extra time. Béziers then won the penalty shoot-out 3–1 to win their tenth French Championship title in 13 years.

So when Cardiff and Leicester reached 26-all at the end of extra time and having scored two tries apiece in their 2009 Heineken Cup semi-final, the crowd of 44,212 and a massive television audience held its collective breath to witness a unique occasion.

The best Welsh and English outfits in the competition had provided an entertaining spectacle in normal time. Leicester had established a commanding 26–12 lead with Julien Dupuy's fourth penalty goal on the hour, having scored two excellent tries through Scott Hamilton and Geordan Murphy. All Cardiff had been able to muster were four penalty goals shared between Ben Blair and Leigh Halfpenny.

The match looked to be moving the Tigers' way when first Craig Newby and then Geordan Murphy were sin-binned. Incredibly, for the six minutes that Leicester had to play with 13 men, they did not concede a score. It wasn't until Newby returned in the seventy-fourth minute that the fireworks really started. Jamie Roberts gave Cardiff hope with a long-distance score in the corner that Blair, with a magnificent kick, converted. Two minutes later Tom James, with a pretty good impression of an action replay of Roberts's try, went over and Blair again converted to tie the scores.

At 26-all, the teams regrouped for 20 minutes of extra time. Both sides were clearly tired and the battle developed into a joust for a goal-kicking position. Leicester came nearer to snatching victory when a desperate dropped-goal attempt by Johne Murphy from near half-way went wide. Anticipating the penalty shoot-out, each side used its bench to ensure their best place-kickers were on the pitch. With a minute left of extra-time, Cardiff brought the former Welsh fly-half Craig Sweeney on for Jamie Roberts, while Leicester took the opportunity to bring back Dupuy (who had been replaced at scrum-half by Harry Ellis) when Dan Hipkiss went off with a genuine blood injury.

And so, with the sides still level on points and tries after 100 minutes' play, the game moved into new territory. The best five kickers from each club were nominated and Cardiff, through Ben Blair, took aim first. From the middle of the 22-m line, Blair banged home the goal to put Cardiff ahead. Dupuy equalised for the Tigers and the scores reached 4–3 to Cardiff before the first miss, Johne Murphy firing to the left of the posts.

Tom James stepped up to take Cardiff's next kick. Success would have sealed the game, but to the home crowd's dismay he copied Murphy and sent the ball wide of the left upright. Scott Hamilton duly equalised for Leicester and the shoot-out moved into sudden death. Tom Shanklin and Aaron Maugher extended the score to 5–5; Richie Rees (with a low effort that just scraped over the crossbar) and Craig Newby (the first forward to kick) brought it to 6–6. Cardiff had used all their backs now and their first forward to kick was the experienced flanker, Martyn Williams. The only forward in Welsh international history to drop a goal in a Test, surely he would not miss?

Williams addressed the ball with a round-the-corner approach, but went wide of the left post. Step forward Jordan Crane, a recent England cap. The Leicester forward, it later emerged, invariably warmed down at Leicester training sessions with a penalty-kicking competition with his back-row colleague, Newby. The practice now paid handsome dividends, Crane sending the ball true for a 7–6 Leicester win that put them into their fifth Heineken Cup Final.

Poor Martyn Williams was inconsolable, despite the sporting commiserations of the Leicester and Cardiff players. In football, the shoot-out is a contest between kicker and 'keeper. For rugby, this event showed that fame or shame rests entirely with the kicker. There is no contest and it is arguably a very painful way of deciding a game, all the blame for defeat resting with one player. Indeed, in the aftermath, many in both the Cardiff and Leicester camps agreed that a further period of extra time until a 'golden point' was scored would have been a better way to settle the match.

SCRAPE TO VICTORY

CARDIFF, FEBRUARY 2010

In the short history of Cardiff's new Millennium Stadium, there has never been an international match like it. With only four minutes to go, Wales were trailing Scotland 24–14 when the most extraordinary winning comeback brought them an unlikely and unbelievable seven-point victory.

The Six Nations match was a must-win game for both countries. Scotland were beginning to establish themselves as a force again in international rugby after several disappointing seasons. New head coach Andy Robinson had steered them to a famous victory over the Wallabies at Murrayfield three months earlier, but defeat the week before at the hands of France meant that winning the game in Cardiff was vital to keep alive hopes of a successful Six Nations season. Wales, too, had lost their opening match of the Championship, defeated at Twickenham in spite of making a promising comeback.

Indeed, Wales had become notorious for their poor starts and nerve-racking comebacks long before this game against Scotland began, so when they went into half-time trailing 9–18 few in the capacity crowd were particularly concerned. Scotland, however, were playing with enterprise and had thoroughly deserved their lead despite losing Chris Paterson and Thom Evans with serious injuries. Their replacements were playing out of position, but seemed to be slotting in smoothly to their unaccustomed roles.

Even when Scotland lost the third of their starting back-three, Rory Lamont going off with a serious knee injury, their hopes received an instant boost when Dan Parks landed a 40-m dropped goal to take their lead to 24–14 with only 15 minutes left on the clock.

But what a chaotic quarter-of-an-hour followed for the Scots. First Scott Lawson was sent to the sin-bin in the seventy-third minute for a blatant offence at a ruck. A minute later Jamie Roberts crossed for Wales, but was called back for an earlier offence. Scotland's troubles, though, were further compounded by an injury to replacement Phil Godman, who left the pitch needing attention to a head wound.

Wales eventually took advantage when, four minutes from time, Shane Williams weaved his magic path around the Scottish defence to send Leigh Halfpenny sprinting over in the right corner. Welsh fly-half Stephen Jones kicked a magnificent conversion from touch to make it 24–21.

As the teams ran back for the restart Dan Parks had to retire injured and, with all their substitute backs used up, Scotland had to send flanker Alan MacDonald on to play out of position while Godman returned to resume as fly-half.

With barely 70 seconds to go, Lee Byrne made a straight break and, faced by Godman, chipped the defender and jumped to claim the ball. As Byrne fell awkwardly to the ground, referee George Clancy ruled that he had been taken out by a trip from Godman and yellow-carded the offender, reducing Scotland to 13 players. The referee awarded Wales the penalty in a kickable position.

A draw was clearly on the cards as the Welsh captain, Ryan Jones, asked the referee if there would be time for another play after the penalty attempt. Jones was told there would be one more play if the kick succeeded, so the captain summoned Stephen Jones for the place-kick and the Llanelli kicker duly squared the scores.

With the crowd at fever point now and a huge television audience holding its collective breath, Mike Blair restarted for Scotland. In the heat of the moment he failed to realise that simply kicking the ball dead would have ended the match, and instead kept it in play by kicking towards the Welsh 22. Wales launched an urgent counter-attack, but when Stephen Jones cross-kicked to his right many thought he had overcooked his effort and that Scotland would recover the ball and clear to touch. But the match had one last cruel twist for Scotland.

Jones's kick bounced wickedly for Scotland and the Welsh forwards were able set up a couple of rucks, which sucked in Scottish defenders. The ball emerged on the Welsh side and was moved left to Shane Williams who dived over under the posts. The crowd exploded with a mixture of joy and relief and Stephen Jones's conversion gave Wales a most unexpected 31–24 victory.

Never before had an international match taken such a twist in its last few minutes and a trawl through the scrapbooks revealed only one similar game in living memory. Met Police lost 21–19 to Bath in January 1970 in a game in which the lead changed hands three times in injury time. Critics that day said that Tony Crowe, a much-respected London Society referee, was enjoying the game so much that he didn't want it to end.

BEST SUPPORTING ACT

GLYNNEATH, FEBRUARY 2010

There was always going to be something special about the Wales–Scotland weekend of 2010. But it is not only the match that will forever be remembered by those who witnessed it: so, too, will the antics of a kilted young Scottish supporter captured on live tea-time television the night before.

BBC Wales Television's flagship news programme, *Wales Today*, went out live from Glynneath RFC at 6.30p.m. on the eve of the game. The club were hosting members of Hawick RFC and several of the Scottish visitors were encouraged to join the show's sports presenter at the top of the programme. As the cameras rolled and the presenter began her introduction, Keith Davies, a Hawick back-row forward who earlier in the season had been a dignified pall-bearer at the funeral of the great rugby commentator, Bill McLaren, dropped his kilt exposing himself to a nation whilst standing next to the BBC Wales weatherman.

The cameras cut back to the Cardiff studio where the programme's anchor apologised more than once for what was described as unedifying tea-time viewing. Welsh rugby fans, however, were rolling off their sofas at what will go down as one of the funniest pranks ever to succeed on live television.

'He's a really good lad and we all think the world of him at Hawick Rugby Club,' said Hawick RFC vice-president Alister Pow afterwards. Welsh rugby-lovers agreed, though BBC Wales were not quite so fulsome in their praise.

A BRUSH WITH THE LAW

THE M4, FEBRUARY 2010

After the Welsh win over Scotland huge celebrations were only to be expected. But for one Welsh player the partying led to headline-making high jinx, a police arrest and expulsion from the national squad.

In the early hours of the morning after the match Andy Powell, the Cardiff and Wales back-row player, took a golf buggy from the hotel where the Welsh side was staying and drove it along country lanes to the M4. Joining the motorway, he proceeded along the hard shoulder for 1½ miles (2.4km), hitting a top speed of 20 miles per hour (32.2km/h) before pulling off at the Cardiff West motorway service station in search of some sustenance.

Passing motorists had reported the incident to police and the long arm of the law quickly caught up with Powell who was arrested at the service station where, full of remorse for his antics, he immediately admitted his guilt and failed a breathalyser test. He later told a reporter: 'I've done stupid things before when I've had too many sherbets but nothing like this. I thought taking the buggy was a bit of fun but when you've had a few too many beers, everything goes.'

Three weeks later he appeared before Cardiff Magistrates' Court. The prosecution reported that Powell had told the arresting officer, 'It was my idea; I'm an idiot I know.' He was fined £1,000, banned for driving for 15 months and expelled from the Welsh squad by head coach Warren Gatland.

International rugby players have committed worse offences without punishment after international matches or on Lions tours in the past, and rugby and alcohol have invariably gone hand in hand. But rugby is a fully-fledged professional operation today and drink-driving is a serious offence. Rugby's powers-that-be no doubt felt that punishment beyond the scope of the courts was also necessary.

After the hearing Powell, whose conduct was straightforward and exemplary from the time of his arrest – like his swashbuckling efforts for club and country on the field of play – offered a full public apology.

COLLECTOR'S PIECE

PARIS, MARCH 2010

The organisers of the fixtures list for the Six Nations Championship seem to have a happy knack of looking into the crystal ball and predicting which match or matches are likely to produce an exciting climax to the tournament. They certainly kept up the tradition in 2010 when the French were in the frame for the Grand Slam as the crowds gathered at the Stade de France for the Saturday evening kick-off of the fifteenth and final match of the season.

A capacity crowd of 80,066 witnessed France beat England 12–10 to take the title and their ninth Grand Slam, but for nearly 79,000 of them something that is usually taken for granted at big matches was missing. There were no programmes available for the general public.

The reason? An original programme had been assembled as usual by the French Rugby Union's publishers in readiness for the game, but when the Union's officials opened the glossy 84-page magazine, to their horror there was a derogatory article about one of the England players. Not wishing to insult their guests, the Union pulped the entire print run, depriving itself and the publisher in the region of 400,000 euros.

The French hastily arranged for a complimentary replacement programme with a print run of 1,400 to be produced to distribute to the media and VIP guests. The 16-page substitute contained a message of welcome, a few pages of colour action shots and advertisements, and a centre-spread listing the two teams. Yet despite its basic content it swiftly became a collector's item with copies of the rare piece immediately commanding an auction price of £50 to £60 in early eBay activity. Given the importance of the match, it is likely to become a much sought-after item for collectors in years to come.

LIKE FATHER, LIKE SON?

BIARRITZ, NOVEMBER 2011

Imanol Harinordoquy was one of the most abrasive, free-running French loose forwards of the first decade of the twenty-first century. He was tough, uncompromising and particularly relished playing against England as fans will recall. One British journalist described him as 'a broth of a Basque boy.'

England-France showdowns in the early 2000s invariably determined the destiny of the Six Nations title and Harinordoquy featured regularly in these important contests. He was a constant thorn in the side to the English who always found him a handful to contain on the field.

He was big, mobile with exceptionally 'soft' hands for one who stood over 6ft 3in (1.9m), and knew how to handle himself when the action turned nasty. He was certainly not a player to mess with. He once broke his nose in a French club clash with Sébastien Chabal, another fiery French back-row forward, yet a week later he was back in action for Biarritz, playing in a key Heineken Cup semi-final wearing a special protective face mask.

Harinordoquy was at his best when letting his playing skills do the talking – as when he scored a sensational corner try against England in 2002 on the way to a Grand Sam in his first season in the French side. But the key to his approach was an attitude that was perfectly summed up in a comment he made shortly after that key win against Clive

Woodward's England team: 'I despise them [the English] as much as they despise others.'

So where did his fiery attitude come from? Well, first and foremost he was a Basque – Basque-speaking with a love and respect for Basque culture and its customs. He was named after a popular Basque folk singer and his rugby talent derived from native Basque sports. He was a gifted pelota player and even ran with the bulls at Pamplona.

But he was also a chip off the old block. The no-nonsense genes that Harinordoquy inherited undoubtedly came from his father, Lucien, a Basque-country cattle-trader who in November 2011 became involved in a strange rugby incident that demonstrated both family pride and an ability to handle itself physically.

The two great Basque clubs of Biarritz and Bayonne – bitter rivals on the rugby pitch – were playing each other in a Top 14 match when a bout of fisticuffs erupted. The bespectacled Lucien Harinordoquy was so incensed by the Bayonne pack setting about his beloved Biarritz team that he waded in from the crowd to join in the punch-up.

As he squared up to Jean-Jo Marmouyet, one of the Bayonne back-row, the crowd roared at the spectacle of seeing the father of one of France's best-loved players join in the fracas. The greying Harinordoquy-senior was eventually restrained by the Bayonne outside-half, Benjamin Boyet, and at length order was restored by Peter Fitzgibbon, a respected Irish referee on the International Rugby Board's elite panel of officials. Fitzgibbon, a fluent French-speaker (albeit with a Munster intonation), was able to defuse the situation. Happily order, Basque pride and the honour of the Harinordoquy family were soon restored.

DAD STOPS PLAY

HERTFORDSHIRE, APRIL 2014

Let's face it, as parents many of us have felt like doing it. You're watching your offspring playing in a junior match at the start, perhaps, of a journey that will one day lead to county, national or even Rugby World Cup honours – only for all those hopes and parental ambitions to evaporate as the opposition trounce your youngster's team. Thirty, 40, 50 points they concede and there's still 20 minutes to go before the agony is over.

It's not a scenario you'd even imagined. Your child's side is demoralised and dejection has overtaken the team's supporters on the touchline. So next time the opposition look like scoring, you decide to take action. You will run on to the pitch and tackle the wing who is about to career down the touchline to score the eighth, ninth or tenth try – that'll show them!

But of course no-one ever does ... except, that is, unless you are watching Fullerians play against Royston in the final of the Herts Shield that brought down the curtain on the Hertfordshire Junior clubs season in 2013–14.

Fullerians, based in Watford, were trailing 64–5 to their north county rivals when one of the club's most loyal supporters reacted completely out of character at the prospect of seeing his son's side concede further points in the Under-16s Cup Final.

As a Royston player looked certain to extend his team's

lead to 69–5, one of the Fullerians' dads calmly stuck his leg out to send the would-be try-scorer flying off course and spare his team an even bigger flogging. The trip stunned players, spectators and officials, who said they'd never heard of anything like it happening in a rugby match before. The referee wisely blew up for full time shortly afterwards, even though there was time left on the clock.

Fullerians began an immediate investigation into the matter and took swift action. They banned the parent from the touchline for six games and told the guilty party to attend a 'safeguarding' course.

RUGBY'S DAY OF DRAMA

ROME, EDINBURGH AND TWICKENHAM, MARCH 2015

The truth is often stranger than fiction. Certainly anyone planning a fantasy finish story for a Six Nations Championship season could scarcely have written a script with more twists and turns than played out on the final Saturday of the 2015 event.

The Six Nations retains the old-fashioned championship points tariff of two for a win, one for a draw and none for a defeat. There are no fancy bonus awards. When teams finish with equal championship points, then the winner of the trophy is determined on good old-fashioned points difference. Moreover, kick-offs on the final so-called 'Super Saturday' of the tournament are staggered – matches do not start simultaneously as is usual for most league season finales.

Super Saturday 21 March, 2015 began with three of the home unions – Wales, Ireland and England – at the top of the table tied on tournament points, each having won three of their first four games. England were favourites for the title because they were the only team with a home game on the final Saturday. They also began the day holding a slender lead on points difference over Ireland, with Wales placed firmly third, the respective margins being 37, 33 and 12 points. Wales, it seemed, were the outsiders for honours.

An extraordinary day of prolonged drama opened at lunchtime with the Welsh chasing down that points difference in Rome's Stadio Olimpico against the Italians. To take pole position they had to first overcome their 25-point deficit and then post sufficient points to stretch both Ireland and England in their efforts later in the day.

Wales made slow progress during a lacklustre first half and, leading only 14–13 at half-time, it seemed they had blown their chances. But in a spectacular turnaround the Welsh scored 47 unanswered points and ran in six tries after the interval, George North grabbing a ten-minute hat-trick to help them to a 61–13 lead with time running out.

Then, with a minute to go, Wales pressed for another score that would have taken them more than 30 points clear of Ireland. Substitute scrum-half Gareth Davies had only to take a pass for a score, but he knocked on with the line at his mercy and Italy counter-attacked spectacularly with a move that culminated in Leonardo Sarto touching down at the other end, effectively knocking 14 off Wales's points difference. Even so, the win still set Ireland the task of beating Scotland by at least 20 points to leapfrog the Welsh and go top of the table.

Ireland urgently set about their business at Murrayfield against Scotland when skipper Paul O'Connell, typically leading from the front, scored the opening try in only the fifth minute. Ireland's goal was half achieved by the interval, when they led 20–10, and they comfortably overtook Wales's points difference when they added a further 20 points without reply to finish up 40–10 winners.

That left England with the daunting job of beating France by 26 points at Twickenham in the Six Nations' final throw of the dice. They went for it from the start, Ben Youngs scoring in the second minute. They led by 12 points at the break but when Jack Nowell went over for their seventh try and the immaculate George Ford landed his ninth goal of the afternoon with five minutes left, England had improved their points difference by 20 and needed only one more converted try to take them ahead of Ireland and land the title.

In an epic climax, England threw everything into all-out attack but failed to achieve the required score and so Ireland were left to celebrate winning the championship title by the narrow margin of six points. The Six Nations had enjoyed its longest day, with the dramas of Rome, Murrayfield and Twickenham gripping more than 150,000 at the three stadia and played out before a record audience of nearly ten million television viewers.

DOG DAYS

OKATO, MAY 2015

Every dog has its day runs the old adage, and some have even enjoyed their moment in the limelight on big rugby occasions.

As far back as February 1873 the Varsity match was disrupted when a member of the Oxford pack, George Podmore, discovered the perils of playing at Parker's Piece, Cambridge's famous cricket grounds. In those days the venue of the Varsity match alternated between the two great educational establishments, and Cambridge put home advantage to good use by winning by a goal and two tries to nil.

Oxford, however, had to play for part of the match without Podmore. He had to leave the field for treatment after he was bitten by a stray.

Even international matches have been disrupted by a canine. Photographs appearing in the *Illustrated Sporting & Dramatic News* after the 1906 England–Ireland game at Leicester's Welford Road show a terrier keeping up with the forwards during a forward rush. The dog must have been more of an inspiration to the visitors, Ireland winning 16–6, but clearly the committee members of the Rugby Football Union were unimpressed. The Leicester club has only staged two England cap international matches since.

It's not very often that a dog or even a rugby match prevails over news of a royal baby on newspaper front pages, but in May 2015 the rugby-match antics of a stray hound in New Zealand even kept first pictures of the Duke and Duchess of Cambridge's second child out of the front-page headlines. The attacking and defensive attributes of a pint-sized pooch during a match between Coastal and Inglewood was the headline news accompanied by a large colour photograph of the incident.

The dog's first entrance had been early in the premier club match before the threat of a burly forward's size-11 boot prompted him to beat a hasty retreat and seek cover. Undaunted, though, he dashed back on moments later with a rabbit in his mouth. At length, one of the Coastal's backs removed the dog from the playing area, but leaving the poor wounded rabbit on the pitch.

Among the spectators was Berny Hall, a well-known Taranaki flanker with more than two-dozen first-class games for the Union to his name and a man obviously well-versed in rural matters. He dealt with the mortally-injured rabbit swiftly and humanely before disposing of the animal behind the grandstand so that the game could continue.

Moments later, however, the dog was back triumphantly displaying the rabbit's corpse tightly gripped between its jaws, disrupting play once again, before finally settling down under a pick-up truck to enjoy his afternoon feed.

WATER BREAK

LONDON, AUGUST 2015

Taking an early shower is usually a euphemism for a red card, a player sent off for foul play, but at the London Olympic Stadium in Stratford in late August, 2015, the expression took on a completely different meaning during a match between the Barbarians and the Samoan national side.

The stadium was due to host a number of matches in the England 2015 Rugby World Cup and this game, the first team sport of any kind staged on the site, was also viewed as a dress rehearsal by organisers for the bigger matches to follow in September and October.

They must have been hoping that it would be alright on World Cup nights because, like most dry-runs, the organisers had an absolute shocker. Arrangements were inadequate for the crowd of 40,000 or so who descended on the Queen Elizabeth II Stadium. The white-shirted stewards, anxious to reproduce the positive aspects that made the London Olympics such a successful event in 2012, seemed clueless when asked by rugby fans for help with directions to their seats.

Queues for tickets, the toilets and the bars left even the best-natured of fans frustrated at the poor levels of organisation within the complex, while newspaper reporters were astonished to find their area legitimately infiltrated by fans who had been sold tickets for the press box. One journalist, contrasting events with those of 'Super Saturday' in 2012 when Great Britain's athletes had hauled in a memorable pot of gold, described the day as 'Shambolic Saturday.'

Once the game kicked-off the crowd settled down to witness an eventful match. Kane Thompson, the Samoan lock, became involved in an altercation with the Baa-Baas' Australian hooker, Saia Fainga'a, early in the match, flooring the Aussie with a right upper-cut that any heavyweight champion would have been proud of. A minute or so elapsed before the television match official decided to intervene by drawing referee John Lacey's attention to the incident. Thompson was duly red-carded for the punch, leaving the Samoans to play with 14 men for the remaining three-quarters of the match.

Then soon after the game restarted, the most bizarre event of the afternoon occurred. It's fair to say that conditions were hot and humid, but never in the history of rugby have ground sprinklers suddenly appeared from ground level to drench the players with an unexpected (but nevertheless welcome) hose down. Four water spouts from the Samoan half of the field suddenly gushed forth, interrupting play for several minutes while grateful players took advantage of the break to enjoy an early shower of a different kind to the one experienced by Thompson. Two veterans in the Barbarians side, Bakkies Botha of South Africa and Carl Hayman, the former New Zealand prop, took full advantage to cool off.

'That was a first for me,' joked Hayman afterwards, but it would have been no laughing matter had the mishap taken place during a World Cup match. Two stadium officials sprinted along the adjacent athletics track before disappearing into the tunnel to switch the water off and ensure the sprinklers were retracted.

Despite the glitches, the crowd enjoyed a competitive match that yielded eight tries, the Barbarians winning 27–24. And there was plenty to iron out for World Cup organisers with barely a month to go to the start of the event, but that, after all, is the point of dress rehearsals.

BRIGHTON SHOCK

BRIGHTON, SEPTEMBER 2015

The highlight of the long-awaited 2015 Rugby World Cup (RWC) in England came on the first weekend of the six-week competition, when South Africa, twice winners of the Webb Ellis Cup, met Japan, who had not won a RWC pool match since 1991. It was the first time the two nations had met at senior level in a full-on Test.

To emphasise the gulf in class between the nations, South Africa had never fallen out of the top eight of World Rugby's rankings, while the Japanese had never risen into the elite order. It was the classic tier one v tier two clash, with the result a foregone conclusion … or so it seemed.

Saturday, 19 September 2015, was a glorious sunny day in the south of England, where the Brighton Community Stadium, one of the country's newest sports venues, was the stage for the tea-time southern hemisphere/northern hemisphere clash. Jérôme Garcès, the highly respected French referee, was in charge.

The match started at a ferocious pace, as the Japanese stretched their illustrious opponents from touchline to touchline and won their fair share of possession from the set-pieces, despite the clear physical advantage enjoyed by the Springboks.

Eddie Jones, the Japanese coach since 2012, had prepared a side that played a unique style of rugby. Its strength was moving the ball at pace and on this occasion his team played to its game plan with perfection. Indeed, it was no surprise when the underdogs opened the scoring after seven minutes, when their excellent full-back and leading points scorer, Ayumu Goromaru, landed a penalty goal.

It was the first score of an incredible, pulsating match in which the lead changed hands no fewer than seven times, and there were three times in the second half when the sides were level – at 19-all, 22-all and 29-all. Neither side ever managed to establish a lead by more than one score.

The Springboks, however, only trailed for 13 minutes during the match and were leading 32–29 when the last play of this exciting match began. It ended with Japan's substitute wing, New Zealand-born Karne Hesketh, diving over in the left corner for a spectacular try after his side had declined the opportunity to kick a penalty that would have tied the scores. Japan therefore finished winners by 34–32 – the biggest upset in international rugby's 144-year history.

It was a wonderful moment for their coach Eddie Jones whose mother was a Japanese American. He had been Australia's coach in their losing RWC Final against Sir Clive Woodward's England team in 2003, and clearly had never forgotten his mind battles with the former England coach, who was a prominent television pundit at the 2015 event.

'If we make the quarter-finals I'm going to retire from coaching,' Jones beamed when interviewed after the victory. 'Then I can just sit back, criticise everybody and be on television, like Clive Woodward. Tell Clive I want to be like him.'

Alas poor Eddie. The tier two nations have cruel turn-rounds in RWC pool stages, and barely four days later his men had to face Scotland, the other tier one nation in their group. The short recovery time was insufficient for a side that had given its all to beat the Springboks, and Jones's tired history boys were trounced 45–10 at Gloucester, throwing open a pool that also included Samoa and the USA.

Jones's side won their remaining matches to finish level

with South Africa and Scotland on tournament points, but third on points difference. It was Scotland's game with Samoa that proved crucial to deciding which nation progressed from the pool stages to the quarter-finals. Scotland scraped home by three points, thanks to a late Greig Laidlaw try that had a touch of controversy about it. Some felt that he had knocked the ball forward picking it up from the scrum that launched his decisive score. Had the officials spotted it, Japan might well have gone through to face Australia in the quarters. As it was they left the tournament early having become the first nation to fail to qualify for the quarter-finals of a World Cup after winning three pool-stage matches.

South Africa pipped Scotland to first place in the group table and they beat Wales before eventually falling to New Zealand in the semi-finals where, it was noted, the 'Boks' margin of defeat – 18–20 – was the same as against Japan. Some argued with arithmetical logic that, had Japan reached the final against the All Blacks, then the Final would have been a draw and gone to extra time.

A Japan–New Zealand RWC Final decided in extra time? Now there's a thought.